World Encyclopedia of Horses

introduction by David Broome

Encyclopedia
of Horses

edited by Maureen Clerkin

octopus

First published 1977 by
Octopus Books Limited
59 Grosvenor Street,
London W1

© 1977 Octopus Books Limited

ISBN 0 7064 0599 4

Produced by Mandarin Publishers Limited
22a Westlands Road,
Quarry Bay, Hong Kong

Printed in Hong Kong

Drawings by David Nockels

Contents

Introduction

DAVID BROOME

The popularity of horses and ponies is growing every year and now more and more people want to enjoy the horse sports and learn the 'horse lore' that used to be known by everyone from necessity.

Horses are beautiful and on the whole very amenable animals. Many people who do not keep domestic pets and have no particular interest in any other animals still find that they have a soft spot for horses. One way in which this is fostered is by the enormous growth of some equestrian activities which come across well on television. Show jumping makes a splendid 'spectator sport' and has now become a very important branch of equestrian activity. This not only makes good entertainment for the public and a good subject for television coverage; it also helps show jumping as a whole. Being in the public eye fosters increasingly widespread interest in what is involved, helps sponsorships and encourages improvements to the quality of the horses and riders right up to the level of the international teams. Racing, of course, has long been a top sport in Britain.

Nowadays many people – and children in particular – come under the spell of horses without knowing anything about them. Riding schools, riding clubs and Pony Clubs are all catering for this upsurge of interest. Horses and ponies do require a great deal of care and attention, and a proper knowledge of them is vital if they are not to be mistreated. This book provides a basic grounding in horse and pony care, and also contains a wealth of additional information, both in the text and in the many beautiful photographs, which will arouse a more general interest in the different aspects of horses and horsemanship.

David Broome

The Family Animal

ELIZABETH JOHNSON

As riding becomes more and more popular all over the world, so an increasing number of families embark on the ownership of a horse or pony that can be ridden by all members of the family. This may sound a slightly tall order, and it can often be difficult to find a horse or pony that is totally suitable for both children and adults to ride and enjoy; however, provided the purchaser is prepared to look around and not buy the first animal that catches his eye, there is nothing to stop him finding the right type of horse. But before ownership becomes a fact, a family should be totally aware of all that is involved. The next chapters deal extensively with the facilities required to keep a horse or pony for regular work, but it can

companionship. A happy horse will be a healthy horse, prepared to give much pleasure to his owners, so he must be kept contented, well fed and well cared for. The extent of the facilities necessary does depend on the type of animal chosen. A hardy native-type pony will require far less cosseting than the more aristocratic breeds. To go from one end of the scale to the other, a Thoroughbred horse will need to be kept in a well-built stable throughout most of the winter, whereas a pony with Connemara, Welsh or other native blood in his veins will live out all year round, given the proper conditions.

Certain types of horses and ponies are unsuited to fulfil the role of the 'family' horse

do no harm to recap on the basic requirements.

The first essential consideration is whether you realize the need to give up a lot of time to the horse or pony and are prepared to do so. A living animal requires attention *every* day of the year, preferably by the owner or, when unavoidable during holiday or illness, by a reliable substitute who will recognize anything that may be wrong with the animal. Having confirmed that you are prepared to spend both time and money on your new purchase, have you adequate space to keep a pony, preferably with others if it can be arranged? Horses and ponies are gregarious and nothing is more miserable than the sight of a lonely pony, head over the fence, waiting for human or animal

or pony. However great the temptation to purchase the flashy Thoroughbred out of a racing stable and up for sale at one of the major horse sales, it must be resisted. Walking round the sale ring, an ex-racehorse may look as docile as any child's pony, but take it out of the hard-working and disciplined environment of a racing stable, and the placid looking animal rapidly becomes a totally unmanageable lunatic, completely unsuited to gentle hacking once or twice a week with pony or riding club meetings, to small shows or to hunting the odd day. Of course, there are exceptions. There will always be someone lucky enough to purchase the original angelic horse at a sale but, on the whole, these sales should be avoided by all but those

LEFT A chestnut and two dun-coloured ponies. Animals with some Welsh pony or Welsh cob blood in them usually make excellent family animals.

ABOVE At the late Bernard Van Cutsem's stable yard at Newmarket, a string of race horses set out for a gallop wearing exercise sheets to keep warm. If the opportunity arises of buying an ex-race horse you should be strong minded and resist it as any animal from a race stables will most likely need professional handling.

experts who succeed in turning so many of these beautifully bred horses into top-class competition and show animals. It cannot be stressed strongly enough that this is a job for experts and not for a family with limited knowledge of riding.

So what is the most suitable type or stamp of horse for all-round work and for the varying demands made by the different members of a family? It is impossible to lay down a set of rules for the ideal animal. There is no such paragon, but by a process of elimination, and a little tolerance towards one or two faults in the conformation of an animal, it is not impossible to find a very nice sort that will give hours of pleasure to its owners.

So that the animal can be ridden by adults as well as children, it will need to be at least fourteen hands high, and this would only suit lightweight adults. If there are tall members in the family, the horse will have to be a few inches bigger. Horses and ponies can vary so much, and while one that measures 14·2hh. and is lightly built may only be able to carry the lighter members of the family, a cobby, heavier built type of the same height may well suit everyone. A pony type with perhaps a good helping of Irish Draught will probably be well built enough at 14·2–15hh. to carry a 12-stone adult, whereas a lighter breed, such as a New Forest type, will only be suitable for lighter riders, especially if the pony is expected to do several hours work hunting or on long rides.

RIGHT An attractively coloured Welsh Cob of excellent type.

BELOW RIGHT New Forest foal suckling.

BELOW A New Forest foal.

The bigger native breeds in the British Isles are the New Forest, Connemara, Welsh Cob, Highland, Fell and Dale. As with all animals there are always vast numbers of horses and ponies with no documented past – they are sturdy, well built, cobby types, and an expert may be able to pick out certain characteristics of one breed or another, but it is the amalgam of the various breeds that gives us the all-round type so suitable for all forms of riding activity.

Any horse kept in a stable and fed on corn and other concentrated foodstuffs will need from one to three hours work every day, with one rest day a week. This type of work schedule is out of the question for many owners, for children will be at school and adults will be working. It is therefore virtually essential that the family horse can take its own exercise in the field; in other words it must be hardy enough to spend most of its time out of doors. Corned-up, stabled horses will become dangerous objects if they do insufficient work, and the pleasure of riding will soon evaporate if the horse is constantly badly behaved. A stabled horse will also require more expensive feeding, while the native type is adapted to survive and do well on natural foodstuffs (grass) with a winter supplement of hay and concentrates when the grass becomes less nutritious.

Horse and Pony Breeds

The most suitable of the British Isles' native breeds for a family animal (because of their size) are the New Forest, Welsh Cob and Connemara, although three of the North Country breeds, the Fell, Dale and Highland, have frequently proved to be suitable when crossed with a lighter type of animal. The latter three breeds have a working history and are still used in remote areas of the country where wheeled vehicles are totally at a loss.

The New Forest pony, originating in the large tract of forest in Hampshire, has developed over the centuries into a sturdy and attractive pony, sure footed over any going; moreover a most important factor in any family pony, it has an equable temperament and is a willing worker. There is nothing more depressing than a lazy pony which needs constant leg work on the part of the rider. On the other side of the coin, there is the pony that 'takes hold' and is far too lively and strong for the average rider. This can be just as frustrating as the slug, but most 'hot' ponies have been made that way by bad riding, insufficient exercise, inadequate schooling and over feeding.

The Welsh Cob, although he may sound heavy and ponderous on paper, is in fact an ideal type for a family horse. Like the New Forest, he is sure footed and very strong and hardy. Cobs have a slightly stuffy reputation, which is totally out of character with the gay and alert Welsh variety. He will enjoy work, do himself well, and invariably look smart and active. He is also an ideal dual riding/driving pony, a useful quality especially now that driving ponies to harness has become very popular. He may be a little on the strong side for young children, but with good schooling and provided that the children are supervised, he should be quite safe with them.

The Connemara too is very adaptable. He has an extremely calm and docile temperament as well as being exceptionally strong and tough. Several famous Irish horses, jumpers, eventers and even steeplechasers trace back to the attractive Connemara in their pedigrees.

Buying a Family Animal

Having provided adequate room and facilities to keep your horse in good condition, you now need advice on buying an animal that will suit your requirements. There are several ways open to a prospective purchaser, but in each case it is always better to enlist the help of a real expert who will understand what you want, and why you want it.

Age is of paramount importance. Many dealers buy large numbers of young, just broken three-and four-year-olds of all shapes and sizes at Irish horse fairs – Ireland being one of the main sources of all-round riding horses – and these are then schooled on and sold. Provided you have the knowledge and experience to cope with the education of a young or 'green' horse, buying from a reputable

dealer can often be very successful. But without such knowledge the venture can end in disaster. The unfortunate animal will never receive proper schooling and its action and behaviour will go from bad to worse. All too often potentially useful and nice-looking animals are to be seen dragging themselves sloppily along, head almost touching the ground, legs all over the place and no sign of any schooling or discipline. Alternatively, you may go to a small gymkhana and see horses and ponies careering madly about, fighting to get away from their rough and ham-fisted riders whose one object would appear to be to travel as fast as possible, usually back and forth over the practice jump, before racing round the ring

in a jumping event. Moreover, lack of knowledge is frequently the cause of much unnecessary suffering, and many of the young horses brought over from Ireland will be sold to totally inexperienced and unsuitable owners. Thus, a young, unschooled horse, however cheap, will be a constant liability.

On the other hand anything over about twelve or thirteen years will only have a limited working life, although you may want to buy a really safe older animal with a view to getting something a little better a year or two later. But in this case, you will have the added problem of trying to sell an elderly animal when you want to make a change. Horses have a curious way of establishing themselves rather permanently in your affections and it is often difficult to part with an old favourite.

It is far better to look around for something between seven and ten years old. By that age a horse should have learnt its manners and be capable of giving pleasure to its rider. Sales should be avoided by all but the most experienced as there is no chance to see the horse on trial and horse dealing has a deservedly notorious reputation. Undoubtedly the best way to buy a horse is the hard way, by searching through the weekly advertisements in the horse magazines and by travelling to see anything that sounds suitable. Again, try and get someone who really knows what you want to go with you. The basic essentials in any horse are a good temperament, a clean bill of health from your own veterinary surgeon and the ability to do what you are going to want. More specifically, the horse should be quiet to handle, used to all traffic and to travelling in a box or trailer and easy to shoe. I always think it is essential to have a horse on a few days trial if the vendor is agreeable. A lot of people are understandably reluctant to let their horse or pony go away for a limited period, as anything might happen, but if at all possible a trial period is the best way of finding out what you need to know about a prospective purchase. If a trial period is not possible, try and ride the horse away from its home environment. An angelic pony can become an unmanageable little beast as soon as it leaves its own field or its companions. Observe also how the animal reacts to being caught, tended to in the stable and its general behaviour. You can learn a lot before you even put a leg across the saddle. A thorough veterinary inspection is essential and no money should change hands until a bona fide certificate has been issued by a vet of your own choice.

A reputable dealer can often produce just the type of animal for which you are looking; he may have several proven horses passing through his yard; and provided you can find out a little about the animal's history, you can often do well purchasing through such a source. You do need to know the dealer, or best of all people who have bought from him

The ideal horse or pony is obviously difficult to find and you must be prepared to

ABOVE A New Forest stallion. Notice the short ears, intelligent expression and the large crest characteristic of stallions.
New Forest ponies can be anything from 12·2 hh. to 14·2 hh. In the nineteenth century alien blood was introduced but now the breed is much improved again and they make excellent all round ponies. There are regular sales of the ponies in the New Forest, mostly attended by dealers.

A pony sale. Many of the native breeds are sold locally, but sales are not the place for the amateur to find a suitable pony.

RIGHT A Pony Club class being held at a rally which shows a collection of workmanlike ponies and their riders. Most ponies go well in simple bits, a snaffle or a snaffle with a drop noseband.

compromise a little. For example, there may be several faults in a horse's conformation which may prevent it from winning show classes (the beauty competitions of the equine world), but will not hamper its performance as a useful riding horse. Indeed, some of the top international horses are frequently not the most handsome examples of the equine race, but they can jump. So be prepared to accept the slightly less beautiful horse in exchange for safety, manners and a considerably smaller financial outlay. It is impossible to specify the amount of money involved in keeping a horse as prices of foodstuffs vary from month to month – similarly, the price of horses and ponies fluctuates tremendously.

Equipment

The term tack covers a wide variety of the leather and metalwork necessary for a horse or pony. However, the basic essentials – saddle and bridle – are all we are concerned with at this point. It is absolutely essential that both articles fit the horse or pony, and fitting a saddle is a job for an expert. There is a large selection of saddles on the market, but do not try and save money by buying a really cheap article; it will not last and will cause endless problems, sore backs etc. – and can be down-right dangerous. A good general purpose saddle is suitable for most riding activities and you should get a saddler to fit it to your horse.

BELOW Two very different but equally well-cared for ponies being ridden through the woods. The younger girl is wearing safety stirrups on which one side is a rubber strap hooked to the top.

There are many other designs, for dressage, racing, jumping, but for normal riding requirements the general purpose will do.

The bridle, consisting of a bit and the accompanying leather work, will vary according to what the horse has been used to and how well he goes in a different type of bit. Many horses will go kindly in the simplest of all bits, the plain, jointed snaffle, a bit with two smooth rounded pieces of metal jointed together. If the horse is apt to open its mouth and resist the bit, a dropped noseband can often help. Frequently you will find a horse that will require something a little stronger than a snaffle and then you can try one of the various bits based on the curb principle. A curb chain acts in the horse's chin groove by leverage on the rein. A Kimblewick bit is often useful on a child's pony that takes a hold and which a child would find too strong in a snaffle. For showing a horse you will need a double bridle, i.e. a snaffle (or bridoon bit) as well as a curb bit, with two reins. This will take a little getting used to for both rider and horse, and will not normally be used for everyday riding.

Martingales, special nosebands and more complicated and severe bits can be used, but if possible the fewer gadgets you have on your horse the better. He will be far more comfortable, will go more freely and be a far nicer ride. Most of these extra bits and pieces are short cuts to avoid basic schooling. Finally, all tack should be kept clean and supple by constant oiling. Dirty, broken tack not only looks bad but is highly dangerous and will probably give way when you are galloping or jumping.

Among the many things to be considered before owning a horse or pony are riding clothes, which are becoming increasingly expensive; but unless you are going to embark on an extensive tour of the shows, you *can* still equip yourself fairly adequately at reasonable cost. Never skimp, however, on your riding hat or on your footwear. Both articles are absolutely essential to your safety. Your hat should be very hard, fit you well (i.e. not fall off at the slightest upset) and conform to the British Standard. If it does not stay on, wear the elastic, and never get on your horse without a hat – whatever the habits of other riders around you. Footwear, too, should be carefully selected: the long rubber riding boots (not Wellingtons) are ideal if you have to catch your horse in a muddy field. Otherwise, short leather jodhpur boots are reasonably priced, and comfortable and safe to wear. A well fitting pair of jeans and a sweater, with an anorak for winter, are the bare essentials. If you want to compete you will have to buy a proper jacket and jodhpurs, and if you want to hunt there are certain rules governing dress which have to be followed.

It cannot be over-stressed that anyone thinking of owning a horse or pony should first learn how to ride well enough to cope on his own with a horse and also know enough about the care and welfare of a living and very demanding animal. If it is a true family horse, the whole family must be prepared to share the work involved and not leave it all to one willing parent. A horse or pony cannot be parked for a week or so, like a car or bicycle. The moment you become an owner, the problems begin. It is a most absorbing and thoroughly rewarding pastime, but one that requires dedication on the part of the owner. Only then will the fun and pleasure of owning this versatile creature become apparent. For rewarding they certainly are. A horse will give so much and ask very little in return. Any child who shoulders the responsibility of ownership will develop an independent character and learn to put the animal first,

A magnificent Arab stallion in an unusual bridle which is so light that it avoids obscuring the beautiful face.

15

always. The problems of keeping a pony can become excessive if, through ignorance, the owner neglects the essentials – feeding, exercise, feet and grooming. Many people, too, think that a horse runs on and on like a car. The sad thing is that horses *will* keep going when overworked. They are basically willing beasts and will work until they drop from overwork and exhaustion.

So it can be seen that keeping horses and ponies is one of the most demanding of any sport or recreation, but for so many it can be a thoroughly satisfying hobby; hard work with the guarantee of pleasure and new challenges every day as horse and rider progress together.

ABOVE The quality head of a well-bred pony with an intelligent and calm eye. He is wearing a German snaffle and drop noseband showing how well this noseband can be fitted :- the band should rest about one inch above the end of the nose bone; if it is lower it may squeeze the pony's nostrils. There are guards on the reins to prevent the rings of a running martingale going up to the bit. The headpiece is unusual as the throat latch and the cheekpiece are separate.

RIGHT A show pony wearing a stitched bridle with an eggbutt snaffle bit. The bit just crinkles the corners of the pony's mouth which is as it should be fitted. The browband allows plenty of room for the ears and there should be room for four fingers underneath the throat latch to allow the pony to flex its head.

Horse Psychology

MOYRA WILLIAMS

The science of psychology investigates the reasons behind the behaviour of animals. These reasons depend very much on the physical make-up and the environment in which the animals are adapted to live, so before one can really understand the behaviour of any animal, one has to study its physique, and particularly the structure of its sense organs.

Vision

Vision, one of the most important senses to both man and animals, is the result of electrical activity in the retina, a layer of cells at the back of the eye; these cells convey impulses to the brain when stimulated by rays of light. The retina of man and of monkeys contains two different sorts of cell; some are shaped like rods, and the others like cones. It is the combination of these two types of cells which makes colour vision possible. A shortage of cones may indicate colour-blindness.

The eyes of horses, like those of most other mammals, contain only rod cells, so it has always been assumed that they cannot see in colour. Recent research, however, may indicate otherwise.

Dr. Bernard Grzimek has published the results of work in which he claims to have been able to train horses to distinguish between colours. Two horses were used in his experiments; each was led numerous times into a riding school in which were a number of mangers filled with oats. A coloured card was hung in front of one manger and in front of the others were cards of various shades of grey. The horses were allowed to eat only from the manger displaying the coloured card; whenever they tried to go to the others they were prevented from doing so. Eventually, when the horses were taken into the arena where the training had been carried out, they would invariably make for the manger with the coloured card and would ignore the others. This indicates, according to Dr. Grzimek, that colour-vision in these animals is possible, even if not very often utilized.

Even if they cannot distinguish colours, there is no doubt that horses can distinguish different shades and textures, and are usually very scared of bright white or dark black objects when these are first seen. The reason for this may not lie with the nature of the colours themselves, but only with their rarity. In the temperate zones of the earth inhabited by horses, completely white objects, for instance, are seldom found in a natural setting. As anything rare is a potential danger, it will typically be treated with suspicion until it is proved to be harmless.

Fear of dark areas may be explained in a different way. It is often found that during cross-country events, the fences which are most likely to upset horses are those which involve jumping out of sunlight into shadows or woods. The reason for the upset is likely to be due to the peculiarities of a horse's vision.

It is only natural to be cautious when entering a dark place from a light one, as there is a temporary blindness which lasts until the eye adjusts to the difference in the amount of light reaching the retina. This blindness is usually very short-lived. The eye, by the process known as dark-adaptation, soon gets used to the situation, and after a short time may be able to see just as well in deep shadow as it did in the sunlight only a few minutes before. The process of dark-adaptation occurs in nearly all mammals and takes place at more or less the same rate in all the individuals of the same species, though the rate differs considerably between one species and another. In humans, the speed is comparatively fast, within a few seconds of coming into a shaded room from the sun outside, the outline of large objects can usually be distinguished and within twenty minutes the whole adaptive process is almost completed. Curiously enough, animals such as dogs and cats, whose eyes are made to enable them to see in the dark, take longer than humans to adapt to sudden changes of illumination. Dogs, in whom the speed of dark-adaptation has been studied most carefully, seem to take nearly twice as long as man, so that if a man and his dog both enter a room at the same time, the dog will still be able to see very little when the man is seeing without difficulty.

It seems probable that horses too adapt very slowly to changes in the intensity of light, as their eyes are also specialized for night vision.

To ask a horse, therefore, to jump from the sunlight into shadow is like asking it to jump into the unknown; and no horse, unless in such a state of excitement that personal danger is forgotten, or unless so completely confident in its rider that it is prepared to do whatever is asked of it, will be at its best in such circumstances.

A very important aspect of vision is that of focusing. Our eyes cannot focus simultaneously on objects at different distances. When an object in the far distance is seen clearly, those closer to hand will appear blurred; when a near object is in focus, the more distant ones are blurred. Yet a normal young person can switch over from near to distant with comparatively little difficulty.

To understand how this comes about, it is necessary to consider the structure of the eye itself. The eyes of most mammals consist of two cavities, each filled with a transparent fluid. They are divided from one another by a layer of opaque, elastic tissue – the iris – in the centre of which is the transparent lens.

Now in order that the rays of light from an object may be bent and brought to form an image exactly on the retina, the lens makes itself round and fat or flat and thin according to the distance of the object from the eye. This process is known as accommodation. As a person gets older and the elasticity of the lens decreases, accommodation becomes more difficult and extra lenses must be fitted to frames in front of his eyes in order to help him overcome that difficulty.

The lens inside a horse's eye has no elasticity or powers of accommodation. The problem of distinguishing objects at different distances is overcome by having the retina arranged on a slope or ramp, so that the bottom part is much nearer the lens than the top part. The only way a horse can focus on objects at different distances is by raising or lowering its head so that the image is brought into contact with the correct part of the retina. For a horse living in the wild state, this is an extremely practical arrangement; while its head is down feeding, both those objects at its feet and those in the distance above the horizon will be in focus at the same time. For horses that are being ridden and driven, however, it means that when they are made to hold their heads up, the objects at their feet will always be out of focus and will only be seen imperfectly. This is probably why horses often shy at close objects, and why, when they are being ridden over rough country or jumps, they should be encouraged to keep their heads low.

The manner in which a horse focuses its eyes must make it difficult for it to judge distances accurately. This difficulty is probably emphasized because horses do not possess binocular vision. There are many ways in which depth and distance can be measured visually. Humans, because their eyes are situated close together on the face, are able to take in very much the same scene with each eye. This is called binocular vision. Since each eye sees the scene from a

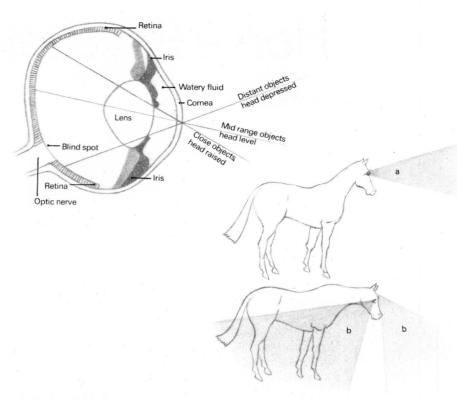

slightly different angle, each receives a slightly different image; the two are superimposed inside the brain and the combined result is a three-dimensional picture. Binocular vision gives objects the appearance of solidity while establishing their position in space.

A horse's eyes are set wide apart on the sides of its head so that each takes in a very different view. Images do not superimpose in the same way as in the human brain. The perception of depth is, therefore, very different for horses and humans. The position of a horse's eyes, however, do give it the ability to see great distances behind as well as in front and also to see each side simultaneously. This wide-screen vision would be a most valuable asset to an animal living on an open plain and subject to attack from any direction – more valuable, perhaps, than accurate depth perception.

Hearing

The sense of hearing is sharper in most animals than in man; but the horse's sense of hearing has never been studied very systematically. We know from experience that horses quite quickly learn to distinguish the commands that are given to them when they are being trained on the lunge (provided that the commands are always given in the same way and are quite distinct from one another). It is also obvious that horses quickly learn to associate the sound of food being prepared with the anticipation of eating it, and that calls between a mare and foal will be recognized by each other. Horses do not respond to their names, even if they are being called to be fed, nor do they seem to use sound very much when communicating with one another. Beyond these few observations there is little really known about a horse's hearing or use of sound. The facts suggest that sounds are not very important to them in their natural elements, as where a sense is unimportant for survival it tends to be comparatively poorly developed. One might wonder why, if this is so, the horse has such large and mobile ears. The reason is probably that the ears are used in place of voice or hands for signalling to one another rather than for focusing sound waves. This point too will be taken up again later when we come to consider communication itself.

Smell

Smell is another of the senses more important to, and therefore better developed in, animals than in man. To what extent horses use the sense of smell, we do not really know, but although horses do not sniff the air as ostentatiously as dogs, most horses, especially young ones, appear to take a keen interest in smells. A youngster is never at home with a new person, in a new stable, or in front of a new piece of saddlery until it has had a good sniff at it, after which it often raises its head and curls up its top lip in a gesture first described by Flehmen, and now often called after him, the Flehmen gesture. Moreover, all horses, young and old, sniff at one another when first introduced.

Undoubtedly the most important use made of smell by those animals in which it is strongly developed is in the sphere of communication and territorial recognition, and it is therefore in this connection that a horse's sense of smell should be assessed.

Most animal species stake out their territories by 'scent-marking' them with their excreta. In horses this is the job of the stallion who will deposit his dung in neat piles at various points over his territory. Intruders will recognize these as the signs of ownership and behave accordingly. On the other hand, mares, and to some extent geldings, spread their dung liberally over a wide area as they move, so that a lost member of the herd or family will be able to find its way back to the group by tracking them from one pile of dung to the next.

In most young horses, even after years of domestication of the species, this tendency is still well retained. A youngster out on the road for the first few times will want to stop and smell every pile of dung it comes across, as if to make sure it is not trespassing. All horses, young or old, retain the tendency to mark a freshly cleaned or newly entered stable in the natural manner by covering it with their excreta.

Finally, smell may have a very important function in telling the horse the state of another individual. The emotions have a strong influence on the body – especially the sweat glands – causing these to start exuding their contents. Hence an excited, worried or fearful animal will give out a distinctive – even if only very faint – odour, which an animal with a well developed sense of smell may well be able to detect. This may be why horses can usually recognize people who are afraid of them.

Touch

The senses dealt with so far – those of sight, hearing and smell – have one very important

function in common. They give the individual information about things that are going on some distance away from him and so allow him to anticipate and, if necessary, avoid danger. But before an animal can really know what different things are like – which are dangerous and which safe, which pleasant and which unpleasant – he has to come into direct contact with them; he has to touch them.

The skin is a highly specialized organ of touch. It is important, therefore, for the skin to be able to tell the animal a good deal about the quality of different objects. It tells the animal whether an object is hot or cold, whether it causes pain, and whether it is hard or soft; exactly how it differentiates between these different sensations – touch, temperature and pain – is still a considerable mystery. One thing only has been established with certainty. Most of the skin is actually quite insensitive, but scattered over its surface are minute spots, some of which will respond to one sense, some another. Thus, a spot which responds to touch will not respond to pain; one that responds to temperature will not necessarily respond to pressure.

Although all areas of the skin have a certain number of these discrete sensory spots, some areas have many more than others. The mouth, the feet and the hands are particularly well-equipped, and are very much more sensitive to touch than, for instance, the middle of the back or the forearm. In addition, some areas concentrate much more on one type of sensation than on others. In man, the tips of the fingers are especially sensitive to light touch and temperature, while comparatively insensitive to pain; the inside of the mouth, however, is very much more sensitive to pain than to temperature. It is possible to drink things which are too hot to hold comfortably in the hand, although a minute pimple inside the mouth will be far more agonizing than a sore of equal size on the finger.

The general pattern of sensitivity appears to be very much the same throughout the entire animal world. The vital areas around the mouth and extremities are always those most richly provided with sensory spots. One has only to touch a young horse around the mouth or try to pick up one of its feet to realise that this is so. But sensitivity may alter with experience. In man, for instance, it is well known that if the sense of sight is lost, the sense of touch becomes much finer – not because nerve endings or touch spots are developed in the skin but because the individual learns to distinguish minute details which, at first, he was inclined to overlook.

That the same thing happens in horses is quite plain to anyone who has ever tried to school them. When a young horse is first backed, it not only fails to understand what is required of it when its flanks and mouth are touched, but it needs considerably more pressure on these parts to make it understand what is required of it than is the case later on. Gradually, with training, the horse learns to

TOP LEFT A schematic diagram of a section of the eye of a horse. Due to its 'ramp' retinas the horse must raise or lower its head to focus on objects at varying distances.

ABOVE LEFT Three diagrams illustrating vision in the horse. When the head is raised the horse will see forward (A); when lowered it will see to the side or rear (B). The horse can see either forward or laterally and to the rear but not the two combined.

interpret and anticipate the different signs and to respond to very much slighter pressure than was originally necessary.

The fact that sensitivity to pressure can become very keen over some areas of the horse's body is not, however, an unmixed blessing, for it is possible that the highly trained animal may finally be able to perceive the slightest and most unconscious tensions and muscular twitches in the rider. The involuntary activities of the body which accompany thoughts and emotions have long occupied the attention of psychologists, and it is now realized that almost every emotion, thought and desire which passes through the mind is reflected to some extent by activities in the body. Although it sometimes takes extremely sensitive scientific instruments to measure the psychological changes, some of them are obvious and familiar. Probably everyone has had the experience of some embarrassing situation during which, at the moment of emotional tension, he has found himself sweating or blushing. Not everyone, however, realizes that the moment he even thinks of an embarrassing moment his heart will begin to beat faster, his hands to sweat, his mouth to dry up, and his muscles to tense, while the more he tries to fight back these tell-tale reactions and appear outwardly calm, the more violent they will become. Even the voluntary and quite unemotional contemplation of some action will produce electrical discharges from all the muscles which would be involved if it were carried out. A person who thinks of striking a tennis ball will set minute electrical impulses passing along all the nerves and muscles which would be involved in the actual act.

Although man himself cannot detect the smallest of these changes except by means of complicated and very delicate instruments, there is reason to suppose that some animals are able to do so with their unaided senses, and that the very slight muscular tensions and movements which accompany anxiety, the expectation of some momentous event, or a bad temper, may be picked up by a horse and arouse similar sympathetic responses in its own body.

Horses also use touch in all intimate contacts with one another. The young foal, like most young animals, makes use of its mouth and whiskers in its earliest explorations of the world. Friendship and trust are communicated from one horse to another by nibbling along the neck and withers; if a human wants to reassure, congratulate or reward a horse he often copies this by patting it on the neck. When a mare is ready to mate, she will lift up her tail and spread out her hind legs when a stallion touches her under her tail or on the side of her flank; if she is not in a state to mate, however, touches in these places will be answered by kicks and squeals. If any other animal – including man – touches a mare in those same places, the resultant behaviour will be just the same as if the touch was delivered by a stallion.

Time Sense

Whether horses have an inborn time sense is still an open question. There is no doubt that they are very regular in their habits and expectations, liking to do the same things at about the same times each day. Are these actions really governed by a sense of passing time or by external cues?

As man himself is sadly lacking in the ability to judge time accurately – perhaps it is for this reason that he has had to invent clocks – it is unlikely that much insight into the matter will be gained from his introspections. To man, the passage of time seems to be a purely subjective

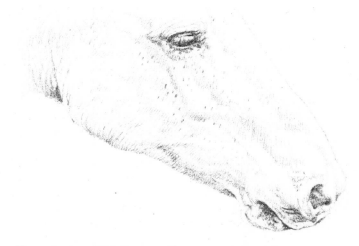

affair, dependent on his expectations and emotions, his occupation and his feelings. When he is busy or when he is hot and feverish, time will pass more quickly than when he is not. An event which is anticipated with pleasure will seem to come more slowly than one that is dreaded, and in retrospect the passing of a few seconds can seem to have taken longer than the hour of which they formed a part. Curiously enough, a person who may be hopeless at judging the passage of a few hours when he is awake may be fairly accurate during sleep, and able to go to bed at night with the perfect assurance that he will wake up the next morning at approximately the desired time.

The difference between the time-sense of man and that of some animals indicates that time is not equally important to all species. Is it really important to horses? Most people would insist that it is. As mentioned, horses do appreciate regularity and if free to do as they please will maintain a routine that varies little from day to day. One summer, I kept careful notes of the behaviour of one group of horses which had free access to a barn and a field. Even on days when the flies did not seem particularly bad, the horses tended to retire to the shelter at about 9 a.m. and leave it again only in the evening at about 6 p.m. Their regularity in this respect gave such an impression of time-consciousness that it seemed sensible to admit to this interpretation. Towards the end of the experiment, however, there was a partial eclipse of the sun. For about half an hour in the middle of the day the temperature dropped, the wind died, and darkness seemed about to fall. Man was not apparently the only creature to have the impression of impending night. The chickens began to roost, cows in the neighbourhood lowed for their milkers, and our horses flicked their tails, shook their heads, and walked out into the field for grass. Four hours or ten hours, the interval as measured by clocks seemed to be immaterial to them; it was the external conditions which had prompted them to eat in this case, not the inevitable march of time.

But whether one is justified in arguing from these observations that it is immaterial at which times stabled horses are fed, watered and exercised is another question.

ABOVE LEFT The horse uses its sense of smell to familiarize itself with new people and new surroundings. The nostrils also express the horse's moods.

ABOVE The horse possesses acute hearing. It can quickly learn to distinguish voice commands. As with the nostrils, the long, mobile ears are used as signalling devices.

Inborn Needs and Urges
As well as having their own specialized senses, horses have very special physiological and psychological needs. The horse is built to survive on large, open plains, to gallop fast in order to escape predators, to travel great distances in search of food, and to live in groups or herds. In the natural state, a horse's food is easily available at any time, so, unlike dogs and other species which have to work for their food, a horse never seems to associate food with any special act it has performed. In fact, it never really looks on a tit-bit as a reward for good behaviour, although, as mentioned earlier, it quickly learns to associate the coming of food with certain sights (such as buckets) or sounds (such as doors being opened). It also quickly learns to associate the presence of good food with certain places or events, so that if a horse originally seems to be afraid of a particular person (such as the vet or blacksmith) or a particular place (such as the inside of a mobile horse-box) feeding it tit-bits in the presence of these horrors will often allay its fears.

Horses are also slow to learn that if food is present at all, it should be shared equally! They will squabble and fight to take first pick, but those which are pushed away never give up trying to snatch their share. For this reason, taking tit-bits into a field full of loose horses can be a hazardous task; in their scuffles, the horses are quite likely to kick or knock over their would-be benefactor, and children especially are often hurt in this way.

Being by nature social animals, horses not only have a great need for company, but also have an elaborate system of communicating with one another. A few of their signals are vocal, and we can recognize these without much difficulty. They range from the low, snuffling whicker of friendship, to the high, shrill neigh for help, or the squeal of anger. Most of their signals, however, are made by gesture. The tail and ears are particularly important for this purpose; when the ears are laid back tight and the tail is swished, the horse is indicating that it is angry and is threatening, but when excited, a horse's ears are pricked forward and its tail lifted high over its back. The mouth and the position of the head are also used for conveying signals. A young horse, for instance, will signify its submission to an older one by the 'snapping' posture. This posture is seen when a horse sticks its head out and up, curls back its lips and chatters its teeth. The expression is like the grin seen in many other species, including monkeys, dogs and man.

Even quite old horses will occasionally revert to this gesture if they are introduced to large groups of strangers and want to avoid being attacked. When, for instance, a mare arrives at a new stud and is turned out to graze with the regular inhabitants, she will often greet them with this posture. Snapping is usually replaced in older horses by other gestures.

Whether the snapping gesture or, for that matter, any signal, is inborn or learned at an early age from other members of the herd, is a question to which no-one really knows the answer. I was able to watch the development of a number of foals which lost their mothers at a very early age, and were hand-reared till they were able to fend for themselves. Those which had been reared in total isolation and saw no other horses until they were several months old failed to make the appropriate gesture of submission when they met strangers, and consequently were badly mauled. Those which were raised in groups, however, even if an older animal was not present to show them what to do, snapped regularly at any stranger, equine or human, and had no difficulty in being accepted by natural groups. It seems as though the communication signals of a species are probably inborn, but are not practised or released unless the animal properly identifies itself as a member of that species.

In horses, the angle of the mouth and lips are extremely expressive and should always be watched carefully. If the animal is tense or nervous, its jaw will be set hard. Once it relaxes its jaw and begins to make chewing movements (similar to our smacking or licking our lips) one can be sure the horse is relaxing and losing its first fears.

One great difficulty is that in all animals the signs of fear or submission and those of anger or readiness to attack are very similar. Perhaps this is not surprising as the emotions themselves often merge into one another. Just as the grin of friendship in monkeys and man is very similar to the grin of fury – only the shape of the eyes is really different – so, in the horse, the submissive snapping of the foal is very like the threat of attack by an older animal. In these creatures it is probably the angle and activity of the tail which gives a better clue than the shape of the eyes. In submission the tail is kept still whereas in anger it is swished from side to side.

In any group of horses – even a group of two, a dominance hierarchy has to be established and accepted so that all the individuals in the group know what their positions are. At one time it was believed that most animal societies were built on a hierarchical system, the grades of which were often seen to be far more rigid and clearly defined than even the most class-conscious human society. Hens are a classical example. Among all confined communities of these birds it will be found that one is the top ranking and can peck all the others, while one is the lowliest and can be pecked by the rest.

In the majority of animal societies, however, including that of horses, the pattern is seldom so rigid. A major difficulty in assessing an individual's position in the hierarchy is to decide which criteria are to be used in measurement. Threats or gestures of anger would seem the obvious ones, but in fact these might be very misleading. The dominant horse is not always the one which most regularly bullies and threatens the others. In my own time I have had two very dominant mares; in each case when out in a field with other horses, the mare had only to flick an ear or quiver her tail for all her companions to flee. When threats were made, it was usually observed that each individual tended to pick on one or two others for special attention, as if deciding that these were his or her particular rivals and that the others did not count.

Although the positions are established by means of threats (and the occasional attack), animals at liberty seldom do one another any serious damage. The weaker or more lowly individual will usually give way at the critical moment, signalling its submission to the dominant one and then turning on one lower down in rank than itself! A very high-ranking animal does not usually bother to threaten a very low one, but reserves most of its attacks for those nearest to it in the hierarchy, those which constitute the greatest danger to its own particular position.

The tendency for family members to stick together and to form special relationships with one another has been noted by many breeders, but exceptions have also been found. In my own experience, mares react to their offspring in as many different ways as human mothers do. One of the first brood mares I had, a grey three-quarter thoroughbred, Nuki, was particularly antipathetic to her own daughters. The oldest of these, Nauri, and the second, Nuit, had both inherited many of her dominant characteristics, so that, when they grew to maturity they were as reluctant to play second fiddle as their mother had been. Perhaps it was for this reason that Nuki saw them as her greatest dangers and felt the need to keep them under her control. Her sons and grandsons, however, were very seldom threatened. Although her daughters were not allowed to approach within five or six yards of her when she was waiting to go through a gate or resting in the shade, she would allow her sons to lean on her without turning a hair.

You may wonder what all this has to do with riding or managing horses, and why any rider –

The angle of mouth and lips are an indication of the horse's mood. The horse below with tense jaws and curled lips is angry. The calm jaw and lips of the bottom one shows contentment.

especially one who merely wants to race or jump his horse – should bother to understand how it lives in the wild or how horses communicate with one another. One good reason is because horses react to signals they receive from any other animals, including man, as if they were from an animal of their own species. In fact, to his horse, a rider is really just another horse, and his horse will test to see which of the two is going to be boss and give the orders. It is important in any partnership that this is quickly established. Of course it is always possible for one partner to be boss in one situation and the other in another but this arrangement is usually clearly defined between them.

Since man cannot give the same signals that a horse can – having no tail to lash or ears to lay back – how is he to communicate his intentions and desires? One good method is by using the voice (the low, staccato reprimand seems to be accepted as such by all species). Another method is by signalling in much the same way as a horse would, that is to say, by waving something (an arm, a rope, or a stick). The horse will often take this as a threat gesture and realize that the man means business. Sometimes a very forceful horse will defy this human threat, just as it would defy the threat of one of its own herd; if the threat is accompanied by a painful slap, however, it will soon learn that human threats are to be taken just as seriously as those of its equine companions.

As mentioned above, it is quite possible for a horse to accept that its rider is boss when they are away from home or in strange territory, but for the horse still to believe that it should be boss at home in its own stable. This is especially common when a horse feels that there is something important to fight about like food. Indeed some horses never seem to learn that man is not a rival for their food and lay back their ears every time a person passes or enters their stable with a bucket.

With the increased physical well-being that results from eating large quantities of oats and becoming very fit, most horses will attempt to rise high in their social hierarchy. This means they will increase the number of threats and challenges they issue to those close to them in the pecking-order. In the case of a working horse this usually means their riders or handlers. Most riders recognize this when they say their horses are becoming 'fresh'; what their horses are doing is testing out their dominance by acting in ways they know to be forbidden, like shying at familiar objects and bucking when they are supposed to trot or canter. The testing-out can be perfectly good-natured and friendly, but if the rider does not respond with a friendly reprimand there is a grave danger that the horse will take this as a sign of weakness or submission on the rider's part and try something a little less harmless next time. In this way bad habits are quickly established.

Just as it is difficult to distinguish submission from anger, so it is often very difficult to distinguish threats of this sort from genuine fear, for once again the two mingle into one another. Sometimes, indeed, an individual himself cannot tell the difference between them, or may feel he has to stand up to and even provoke a fight with the object of his fear, in order to see how strong he is himself. Hence, if a young horse stops when approaching a stream, a noisy vehicle or a brightly coloured obstacle, it is not always easy to tell if this is because of fright or just because it is testing-out its rider. If it is really frightened, severe punishment could be fatal to its future development, by turning something which was only marginally feared into a source of real terror. If, on the other hand, it was really just being defiant, punishment could prevent an act which started as a simple test of dominace becoming established as a bad habit.

From what has just been said, it is clear that there is another very important factor which determines and regulates behaviour – namely learning. Horses, like all animals, start learning – that is to say, modifying their innate behaviour patterns in the light of experience – from the moment they are born; but the way they do so and the things that influence them most are not the same as in man. Like man, they do show three different types of learning – perceptual learning, association learning and motor learning – and each of these has a very important effect on their adult behaviour.

Perceptual Learning

The young foal is born with its eyes closed but almost immediately they are opened, so that from the first moment of its life it is able to register everything that it sees. The human child, on the other hand, is unable to recognize another human's face till it is some weeks old. Perceptual learning can proceed in two different ways: differentiation (that is learning to tell the difference between two things even if they are alike in a variety of ways – the difference, for instance, between a daisy and a buttercup), and generalization (which is learning to recognize in what ways things are alike and can be grouped together overlooking their differences – to recognize flowers because they grow, and have green leaves, or animals because they move and breathe). Man is good at learning by generalization, but finds differentiation more difficult; the horse while excellent at differentiation is very poor at generalization. A foal will recognize its home territory after a single day in it, and if anything is changed there, or if it is asked to move away, shows definite concern. If, however, a potentially frightening object such as a white barrel, which it has learned not to fear in one position, is moved to another place, it evokes just as much suspicion as on the first occasion. A familiar shape – even that of a well-known companion – will be treated as completely new if it is altered in any respects. I well remember the absolute panic which was aroused in one group of young horses the first time one of the older ones was dressed-up and turned out with them in a New Zealand rug. The youngsters had been grazing with and along-side this particular veteran for months before the autumn frosts were considered cold enough for the old thoroughbred to need protection. When it appeared among them in this altered guise, the young horses treated it as a complete stranger. One of them made repeated threats and mock attacks – alternating these with dashes for safety – until it finally dared to approach near enough to recognize its mistake. Even familiar objects appearing suddenly in the home field or stable for the first time will be treated with intense suspicion, but perhaps the most difficult thing for us to understand is that something can appear different to a horse if the thing itself is not altered at all but the horse's own situation is changed.

A particularly vivid instance of this occurred when I was first schooling Gambit, a horse which went on to become an international show jumper. Gambit, at that time, was sharing a field with his father, Gamesman, whom I was preparing for his first show jumping venture. I had only one jump to use for schooling at that time and it was a homely affair composed of tin barrels situated in the field where the two horses were spending their evenings together. Both horses had been schooled to jump these barrels and did so without any fear. In order to make them more impressive and also to accustom Gamesman to the colour, I one evening took a bucket of whitewash up into the field and began to paint the barrels. Both horses were intrigued by my antics, especially Gambit, who did all he could to help or hinder my efforts by licking the wash off as fast as I put it on. The next morning I saddled him and rode him up into the same field, but he behaved as if he had never seen the barrels before. He would not go within twenty yards of them without snorting and shivering with fear, and it was not until I had laid them all down on their sides and made him walk along between them that he finally consented to jump over them. He had jumped them uncoloured without any trouble and he had seen them coloured. But to jump them coloured was something apparently, to him, quite new. One might say this is like altering the angle from which an object is viewed. Although man can be very misled if the visual angle of an object is changed, he would not expect his perception of familiar objects to change each time his situation while viewing them was altered; to see things differently when, for example, going to work, and differently again when visiting friends!

All these instances may give the impression that the horse is incredibly stupid, and indeed, this is often held to be the case. Because man is so good at generalizing and so poor at discriminating, we tend to equate intelligence with generalization, or abstraction. But to survive in its natural habitat, it is clear that discrimination is more valuable to a horse than generalization, so we should be careful in our judgements!

It is very important for a horse to pick out any slight changes in its environment which

The horse on the right is threatening that on the left. Note the position of the tails and ears.

might betoken the presence of enemies. Things may remain unchanged in many respects but, because of very slight variations, turn from being beneficial to poisonous. This is particularly the case with some plants which may be nutritious at some times of the year but poisonous at others. A horse which was not alert to these changes would soon be dead!

Clever Hans

An interesting case of a horse's brilliant powers of discrimination was that of Clever Hans, a horse which created a great stir in scientific circles at the beginning of this century. A German of considerable repute, Herr von Osten, claimed to have trained a horse to answer questions, tell the time, be capable of four different methods of arithmetical calculation, and many other feats suggesting that it had powers of reasoning and abstraction little inferior to those of man. The problems could be given either verbally or in writing, and Clever Hans, as the stallion was called, would tap out its replies on a board at his feet, using one foreleg to denote the tens and the other to denote the digits.

The claims of Herr von Osten and the behaviour of Clever Hans aroused such interest and raised so many points of philosophical interest, that a committee of eminent scientists was established to investigate the matter. They were given every support and co-operation by von Osten himself and in the end they concluded that there was no trickery or fraud. Shortly after this, however, a private investigator exploded the secret. He asked the horse questions whose nature was unknown to the men present, bar himself. The investigator discovered that under these conditions the horse was powerless to do even the simplest sums or solve the most elementary problems. Indeed, Hans gave the impression of being far more interested in the questioners than in the question. The investigator therefore turned his attention away from the horse and on to the behaviour of the people in charge of him. Close scrutiny finally revealed the fact that the

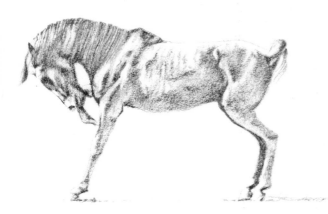

humans were making slight, almost imperceptible and completely unconscious movements with their heads or bodies each time the horse was due to stop tapping. It became clear that the horse had learned to pick up and interpret these movements and not that he had worked out the problems for himself.

Herr von Osten had attempted to prove that horses were intelligent by showing that they could think in the same way as man, solving the same sort of mathematical and logical problems. When Clever Hans' secret was discovered, Herr von Osten's faith in him was shattered. The gentleman failed to realize that it required a very clever animal indeed to make the minute discriminations shown by Clever Hans in interpreting the nods of the attendants. While the horse may have been unable to solve the problems set him by the examiners it was solving one far more important to its own well-being – the problem of pleasing its owner.

Association Learning

The second type of learning is that of association. This is the recognition of the relationship between signs and events, of what signals demand what acts, and of what questions demand what replies. This sort of learning depends largely on repetition. If A is followed by B on several occasions, one comes to expect B every time A appears. Horses, like other animals vary greatly from one another in the speed with which they form associations – another aspect of behaviour which is often taken to reflect intelligence. Some animals seem to grasp the importance of a signal at once; others require constant repetition of signal and response before they begin to show signs of realizing that they are related. These differences are particularly noticeable to trainers, who usually relish the quick learners, the 'intelligent' ones – and become impatient with the slow learners.

Quick learning is not, however, an unmitigated blessing. In horses especially it has its disadvantages. Individuals who are quick to learn one thing are usually quick to learn another also – and this can mean bad habits as well as good. A horse which realizes what is expected of it but which does not want to do it, will often try various evasive tactics; the quick learners will very soon adopt any evasions that prove to be successful. The individuals which are slower to learn are often much more reliable in the long run; for habits that do eventually become ingrained are less easily eradicated or modified.

This became apparent to me in the contrast between two horses, both of which I had bred and of which I was particularly fond. The mare, Nauri, was very quick to learn what was wanted of her. The process by which she did so was fascinating to watch. Each time a new order was presented to her, she would run through all the patterns of behaviour she had learned in the past, keeping her eyes and ears constantly fixed towards me, waiting for the signal that would tell her she had done the right thing. As each act in her repertoire drew the response no, she would drop it quickly and try another. When all of her previously learned actions had proved wrong, she would try new ones until, eventually, she would hit upon the right response and receive my praise. When she had been duly rewarded, Nauri would give a skip and jump of delight and for the rest of our session she would pay no attention to me at all!

Not all horses are, however, as quick to learn as Nauri. Her own half-brother, Gamesman, was by comparison, a veritable dunce. Every new act or new situation had to be repeated over and over again before he seemed to grasp what was required of him. More often than not he would do the right thing by accident, giving the impression that he had grasped what was wanted but the next day or some days later behave again as if the previous lesson had never been given.

These two horses continued throughout their lives to be just as different from each other as they had been in their youth. Nauri could never be relied on to do a job consistently. She was always trying out some new tactic or finding a new bogey. Gamesman, on the other hand, was as stable as a rock. One came to know exactly what he would do in any situation, and to know that if he had done a thing ten times before, he would continue doing it as long as it had to be done.

Motor skills

The third type of learning, that of motor skills, is the most important one to horses, although it is probably the least important one to man. The horse depends for its survival on its own physical prowess rather than on the mechanical gimmicks invented by man to support his rather mediocre physical accomplishments! To refer to a horse's running or jumping ability as a motor skill might at first seem rather odd. In man, whose survival has come from the development of manual dexterity, the term motor skill is usually confined to the things we do with our hands; but the athletic feats of the gymnast, the tennis player, or the figure skater are just as complex; and their acquisition is quite comparable to the learning required of the dressage or racehorse, or the show jumper.

One tendency very marked in horses is that of repetition. If a horse has done a thing once, it tends to do it again; so if a sign or signal has elicited a certain pattern of behaviour once, it will do so again on all subsequent occasions – unless a very great effort is made to alter it, or unless, as in the case of Nauri, the horse is simply trying to be difficult. This tendency is not nearly so marked in other animal species; in rats and monkeys, for instance, the very opposite is the case. If a rat or monkey is faced with a T-junction and turns right the first time, it will almost certainly turn left the next, as if exploration is more important than safety. But in the case of horses this is not so at all. If the

leg and arm muscles of a rider may change his command signals so much that the horse can be confused. Although the difference might be indistinguishable to another human, they might seem immense to a highly sensitive horse, which, in these circumstances, would find itself being given signals it had never received before and would not know how to interpret.

The second point to bear in mind is be absolutely regular with the rewards or punishments which follow your signals. If a horse is patted for jumping a fence well the first time and jabbed in its mouth the second time, it will not know what to do. Once again it will have a sense of uncertainty and insecurity. If this situation is established it may well respond as a human would when he is weary of trying to make sense of contradictory orders and, frustrated, does the first thing that comes to mind – no matter how rash. The horse

right-hand turn has not led to any dire results, it will be repeated every time. The horse's repetition tendency is an important thing for trainers to bear in mind, and the importance of ensuring that the first response elicited by a signal is the desired one will be evident. Most experienced horsemen know this, and may, when buying a new horse prefer to take one that has been completely unhandled rather than risk the danger of taking on a half-trained animal that has already learned bad habits.

In order to ensure that behaviour is shaped in the right way and bad habits are not established, two principles may well be borne in mind. The first of these is be sure that all signals (which include vocal commands, hand signs or touch aids) are clear and distinguishable from one another. One of the most difficult and unnerving things for any animal is to be unsure of what is expected of it. Horses, as I have already pointed out, are very good at distinguishing minute visual differences from one another; but whether they are equally good at distinguishing sounds and touches, we do not know. This may well be so, and may be why a rider who is tense and anxious can convey his feelings to his horse. Tension in the

may merely adopt a defensive strategy and try to gain some comfort from that. The defensive strategies most often taken up by horses are rearing, or napping (that is to say, rushing off back to their home field, their stables, or their companions), but individuals have been known to try all sorts of tactics.

It is common at some of the small county shows to see poor horses and ponies being ridden and even asked to jump by riders who are either so rough or so incompetent themselves that the animals may be certain that, whatever they do, they are going to suffer! If they refuse or knock the fence down, they are going to be beaten; if they jump and do their best they will receive a jab in the mouth and a thump on the loins! It is not surprising that many of them become bad-tempered or nappy: it is only a surprise that so many of them go on, year after year, putting up with it and still doing their best to please!

There are many ways in which a horse can be encouraged to respond instantly and correctly to a signal. The trainer could wait until the horse is already doing what he wants it to do and then give the signal accompanied by a reward. (A vocal 'good boy' or a scratch on the

Stages in the jump.

26

neck are just as effective as tit-bits.) If the required act and the signal are combined often enough, they will soon be associated with each other in the horse's mind. The trainer should also give reward or encouragement as soon as the horse begins to do what he wants it to do, even if the act is not perfect at first. Once the horse knows what is expected of it, skills can be perfected gradually. Finally, a trainer should never expect more of the horse than it is easily capable of doing at the time. It stands to reason that when a horse is being taught to jump, it will not be asked to clear an enormous coloured wall on the first day. It will be introduced to jumping with very low, unfrightening obstacles which can easily be taken in the horse's stride, and only when absolutely confident over these will it be taken on to larger jumps. The same principle holds for every other sort of training, whether it is

he may try again and finds to his amazement that the horse responds correctly at the first touch as if it had been doing it for years. It only needed a break from the constant repetition for the learning to be fixed in the horse's mind.

Would the same results have been obtained without the struggle of the previous session? Could the rider have spared both himself and his horse some anguish if he had buried his pride and given in earlier? The answer is almost certainly 'Yes'. Moreover, by stopping before tempers become too frayed, the rider would not only have saved himself much pain, but would have avoided the risk of upsetting his horse. There is always a danger that an animal which loses confidence, instead of absorbing its lesson at however elementary a level, may resort instead to some unwanted defence mechanism.

introducing a young horse to traffic or getting it to fulfil its potential in a competitive sphere.

One might think – and indeed it is often believed – that the more often and more quickly an act is repeated, the better it will be learned and retained and that if a skill is not practised constantly there is a danger of it being forgotten. To some extent of course this is true; practice does make perfect and long delays do lead to forgetting. A rest of some hours between learning sessions, however, often leads to quicker and more reliable learning than that which is gained from concentrated work. This fact has been demonstrated repeatedly in many different species. A rest immediately after a difficult task has been absorbed is far more beneficial to learning than repeated practice. Much can be gained, therefore, by letting the horse relax – even by turning it out in a field for an hour or two – after a schooling session. A rider may struggle without success for an entire day to teach his animal some simple manoeuvre, refusing to stop until the horse has made a response, however elementary, in the right direction but, in the end, exhausted and exasperated, he is forced to admit defeat. The very next day, perhaps, or even a week later,

Emotional State

The speed with which an animal learns, and the excellence with which it will perform at any given moment, are closely dependent on its emotional state. This state is basically dependent on various biochemicals circulating in the bloodstream, whose function is to speed up the rate at which impulses pass from one nerve to another, controlling the rate at which all the bodily functions take place. In states of rest or relaxation, many biochemicals are stored in various glands, and only the minimum amount required to keep the body functioning at a normal pace is freely circulating in the blood. If danger threatens, or if for any other reason the individual needs to be aroused (for example, in the mating season) messages will be conveyed through the sense organs to the appropriate glands, and large quantities of their stocks will be set free. The product of each of the different glands throughout the body has a rather different function and effects different activities: one causes the bowels and bladder to contract and so rid the body of waste; another causes the heart to beat fast; a third causes the iris of the eye to contract (hence the narrow eyes of the angry animal). Others make the blood vessels contract so that if the animal is wounded it will not lose too much blood. Still others increase the rate of breathing and so enable the animal to work faster while the sweat glands start moistening the skin to counteract the extra body heat.

All these things can be seen easily and will tell an onlooker that the animal is prepared for action. Some changes take place at times of arousal which are not easily seen but which can be deduced from some of the experiments which have been carried out in recent years. One of these is that the brain functions much more quickly at these times than it normally does. Just exactly how the brain works, we still do not know (nor do we know whether it works in exactly the same way in all the different species of animals), but we do know that in states of arousal it produces more alternative responses and produces these quicker than in states of relaxation. It also tends to retain in memory the events which occurred when it was emotionally aroused, better than those that occurred when it was not.

This state of arousal or emotional tension is excellent as long as it only continues for the duration of the emergency and then subsides, but if it lasts for much longer than it is needed it can be injurious to the animal. During the state of arousal, two processes will be taking place. In the first, the body will be using up great reserves of fat and sugar which may soon be exhausted. In the second, the biochemicals which regulate the activity of the nerves themselves will become depleted, and this loss can only be made good by a period of rest and relaxation. Thus it can be seen that efficiency, both physical and mental, accompanies excitement in an inverted 'U' shape. At first there is a gain of efficiency as the emotional excitement increases, but if the excitement continues to increase beyond a certain point, efficiency begins to drop. This is why an animal which is in a permanent state of anxiety or high excitement tends to lose weight and can very quickly be tipped over the edge into thoughtless panic. Each individual has its own optimum level of arousal, for maximum efficiency, and this will depend on its basic emotional state. The phlegmatic, slow, passive character who learns slowly and never bothers to do more than it must, may show a marked improvement if transferred to a new environment; the more highly-strung, suspicious one, who always fears the worst may be tipped over the edge into blind stupidity by such a move.

This may be one of the reasons why horses often respond in quite different ways to changes in their environment. Take two young horses making their first expeditions to the exciting world of the hunting field or the show ground! It is quite common that the one which was very quiet, obedient and docile at home suddenly becomes almost unmanageable, while the one which at home was jumpy and nervous becomes completely subdued. In these cases, it is not only the initial reaction to the exciting new situation which may vary but also the changes which occur when the situation becomes increasingly familiar. The horse who is usually quiet and whose basic level of arousal is low was stimulated by the excitement but will probably revert to its basic quiet state at the second or third outing. The excitable one, whose basic level of arousal is high was stunned into unresponsiveness by the extra stimulation, but may become more and more fractious as familiarity decreases its added stimulation load, and frees its muscles for action.

Temperament and Personality

The difference in arousal-level described above may be one of the factors which determines equine temperaments and personalities, but it is obviously not the whole story, for no two very quiet or excitable horses are exactly alike, any more than two quiet or excitable people are. What, then, is the cause of these individual differences?

Two important factors can be deduced from previous sections of this chapter. These are, first, that there are some needs and urges with which the individual is born and which it derives from its parents by genetic means; secondly, variations may occur in the ways in which these were satisfied in early life.

Many of the differences are associated with – and indeed arise from – the shape and size of the body. The large, heavy Shire, for instance, needs a great deal more food than the small pony: the tough Northern horse with its thick coat needs less external heat than the thin-skinned Arab.

As well as these obvious differences of size and hair texture, there are even more important differences in types of metabolism. The thoroughbred which has been line-bred for speed and excitability, needs a diet much richer in protein than the native pony which has been line-bred for survival on exposed hillsides. The thoroughbred, which receives its rich food mainly from a human attendant will almost certainly develop a different attitude to humans than the hill pony which, although it may be hand-fed just as assiduously by a human attendant in its youth, does not have such a basic physical need for rich food, and therefore fails to associate the human with satisfaction.

While there is almost certainly some relationship between gross temperamental types and physical builds, there is less certainty about the relationship between coat colour and temperament. The advocates of the existence of the relationship will swear unequivocally that all chestnuts are 'hot', blacks 'unreliable' or 'vicious', greys 'docile' and so on. Large-scale studies of wild ponies and horses do seem to indicate that such a relationship does exist, but these scientific studies do not claim that every chestnut will be hot and all greys docile. What they do show is that a large proportion conform to the stereotypes suggested by their pigmentation. If this is so, the question must be asked, why does pigment affect temperament?

So far no-one has produced an entirely satisfactory answer but one possibility which has been suggested (and still awaits a convincing proof!) is that the distribution of blood vessels and peripheral nerves may vary with pigmentation. People in charge of stables know to their cost that horses with white feet and legs tend to give endless trouble. (There is an old horse dealer's saying, 'One white foot, buy; two white feet, try; three white feet, doubt: four white feet, shoot!') The white hooves tend to crack and break; the white stockings are most susceptible to wet. This seems to be because there is a dearth of nerves in the tissue to keep them healthy and combat infection.

If the whole surface-area of a grey horse is equally lacking in nerve cells, the grey horse would doubtless be less sensitive to the touch aids of its rider than a darker horse would be, and any untoward message it might be given due to the riders' tension would fail to reach it. This may well be the origin of the so-called docility of greys, and one reason for their preponderance among children's ponies. The chestnut, on the other hand, usually has very fine, silky hair; this might give the nerve-endings little protection from the rider's touch signals and so make the animals extremely sensitive to slight variations in a rider's aids.

In contrast to their poor sensitivity to touch, grey horses seem to be much more sensitive than darker ones to slight visual stimuli, and can see distant objects, especially in poor illumination. It is the grey which can usually be found standing guard at night and leading the herd in flights from predators.

Another difference which tends to be inherited is that of social dominance. All the

A tense, fearful horse.

offspring of a bossy, dominant mare tend to follow in her footsteps and although it is unlikely that any of them would be able to challenge their dam for leadership, indeed, she would take great care to keep them in their place, they would, if placed among another group, tend to show the same dominant qualities as their dam. (It has already been mentioned that horses tend to treat their riders or handlers as they do other horses, so a naturally dominant horse will constantly test its rider in the same way as it would test an equine companion. Hence the importance of being alert to this characteristic). Whether the family characteristics of dominance are carried on by inherited genetic tendencies, or are due to the youngsters copying the sort of behaviour they have seen to be successful, it is difficult to say, but there is a very strong possibility that innate physical constitution plays a part. As already said, social dominance is closely related to physical well-being and the animal which, because of its genetic make-up, turns its food to good physical use is more likely to succeed in the social hierarchy than the one which uses it to cope with its anxieties!

In pointing out, and trying to explain, these differences between temperaments, I am not suggesting that one is better than another. On the contrary, just as it takes all sorts to make a human world, it takes all sorts to ensure the survival of an animal species. If all the members of a herd wanted to lead it, the individuals would quickly destroy each other in their battles for supremacy. If all the individuals concentrated their sensitivity in the skin, there would be none to save the herd from night marauders. Perhaps it is one of nature's wonderful built-in security measures that coat colour in horses is one of the most unpredictable features of a mating. Although treatises have been written on the subject and statistics may indicate a high probability that a grey mated to a grey will produce a grey foal, there is still a chance that the results of your own careful selection will prove to be the exception and turn out to be bay or chestnut! If it does, do not be too disappointed. It may not suit you, but it will almost certainly suit someone else: for another of nature's marvellous security measures is that there are just as many differences of temperament among humans as there are among horses and the equine temperament that suits one human may not suit another. For an owner and his horse to be compatable it is very important that their temperaments should mesh, and this is a matter which only they can decide. It is extremely difficult, therefore, for one person, however knowledgeable he or she may be in the equestrian world, to choose a horse for another; although the selected mount might be absolutely right for the rider in all logical respects (i.e.: size, shape, ability, experience); if the two do not really feel for one another, the match will be disastrous. On the other hand countless heart-warming instances can be observed of people who own creatures which other people might think useless, but who are devoted to their charges and forever making excuses for their shortcomings.

Vices

In contrast to the different individual temperaments described in the last section, some horses develop unpleasant and generally undesirable habits commonly known as vices. These may occur under saddle (bucking, rearing, napping) or in the stable (crib-biting, wind-sucking, weaving).

Bucking may be of two kinds; bronco-bucking, in which the horse puts its head down, humps its back and kicks up its hind legs, or fly-bucking, in which the head is held up and the back hollowed while the legs are kicked up. In rearing, the horse stands on its hind-legs and lifts up the front ones. In napping it refuses to leave a place of sanctuary (either its home or the company of other horses) and bucks, rears, or kicks if pressed to do so. Not all bucking and rearing are of the kind which would qualify as vices. The most well-mannered of horses can occasionally hump its back and kick up its heels when feeling particularly skittish or when letting off steam – perhaps because it has been confined too long without exercise. After its brief display of exuberance it will usually return to its usual pattern of behaviour. (Some well-known show jumpers and race horses on TV do tend to indulge in a few light-hearted fly-bucks either just before or just after making a great physical effort. The tendency has obviously become a habit, but does not interfere with the animal's ability to perform its job adequately). In the same way, horses may well stand on their hind legs for a few seconds without being classed as rearers. These acts should only be considered vices if they are persistently repeated and prevent learning of behaviour which would be more advantageous in a particular situation.

This last statement gives a clue about the origin of vices, for most vices do start as evasion tactics which have possibly been successful in one instance in early life and then repeated until they become a constant feature of the animal's repertoire. The danger of defensive strategies being adopted in moments of stress and perplexity has already been discussed in the section about how animals learn. Most of the common vices that appear in riding horses begin in this way. Like the tics or compulsions of the human neurotic, they eventually become a kind of mental prison.

Of the stable vices, the commonest are, as mentioned above, crib-biting (in which the horse fixes its teeth on a firm protuberance such as the manger or the top of the door and flexes the muscles of the throat in short, sharp spasms), wind-sucking (the same stance is adopted but without fixing the teeth; at each spasm air is gulped in and swallowed); and weaving, in which the horse stands swaying from one foot to the other, moving its head from side to side. Although these habits are most commonly seen in stabled horses (and seldom seem to appear spontaneously in horses which have not been stable-kept), they may be carried on outside the stables by those animals which acquired them.

How the stable vices originate is uncertain. Boredom has often been blamed for their appearance, and indeed a stabled existence is a most unnatural one for an animal that was designed to spend most of its life in action searching for its food. Unless a horse has plenty of exercise and plenty to occupy its mental resources, its energy will have to be expended somehow and it may well develop unwanted and unnatural methods of letting off steam.

Heredity is another factor which is often blamed, and there is some evidence to support it. This does not mean that all the offspring of a mare or stallion will necessarily develop the same vice as their parents, but two things may be inherited: the first is the level and kind of stress which the individual finds intolerable; the second is the tendency to respond to stress in a particular way.

Stress

Stress-tolerance is a difficult concept for everyone to grasp, because situations which one person might find stressful could leave another unmoved, and vice-versa, but there are some generalizations which can be made. The situations which lead to mental stress can be grouped under three headings (1) conflict, (2) uncertainty and (3) lack of escape.

In the case of conflict, there is a situation or stimulus which arouses two opposing emotions or desires at the same time; the animal cannot choose between them. If, for instance, it is very hungry, the sight of food will encourage it to make for the food-source as quickly as it can. Supposing, however, it sees something else at the food – possibly a very domineering member of its group – which will certainly kick it if it tries to go too close; it will be in a state of conflict (should it approach or run away?) until either its fear or its hunger predominates and decides the issue for it.

In the sort of situation described above, and in most of those occurring in a horse's natural environment, conflicts are usually short-lived or can be avoided, but in the unnatural environment of the working horse, this is not the case. Being constantly asked to do things which arouse some normal anxiety and fear, and yet punished if it does not do them, the poor horse must spend a good deal of its early life in a state of conflict. Its need for human reassurance to minimize its discomfort will be clear, and yet what might seem paradoxical is that very severe punishment for initial reluctance to obey commands can be quite a relief to it by forcing a decision and releasing it from the pressure of the conflict.

It is in a case like this that severe punishment is more likely to solve a conflict than mere threats, and if meted out only for unwanted acts, such punishment seldom leads to neurotic or vicious behaviour. Just as a child soon learns to avoid putting its hand in the fire once it has

Not all bucking is a vice. It can be the result of exuberance after being confined for too long.

been burned (and does not necessarily develop a phobia for fires because of one such experience), so a horse, if it has been severely punished for doing something, will usually just avoid doing that thing again.

What does worry horses and soon makes them very neurotic indeed, is being unable to distinguish whether a situation or a response demanded of them, is one which will lead to punishment or reward; this is the second of the stressful situations – uncertainty. I have described in a previous section the importance of making one's riding signals very clear to the horse so that it knows just what is wanted of it the whole time. If this is not done, it may well be put into a state of conflict and uncertainty; if it cannot tell whether it should stop or go, turn right or turn left, it will not know what to do in order to avoid punishment.

There are situations, however, in which an individual knows that whatever it does, it is going to be punished. These double-bind situations without possibility of escape, can be the most distressing of all, unless the punishment expected is fairly mild and can, therefore, be tolerated. The horse or pony which knows it is going to be jabbed in the mouth if it jumps but hit if it does not is in just such a situation.

You may be wondering what all this has to do with heredity, and especially how it explains stable vices. It is easy, you may think, to see how working situations could produce conflict, uncertainty and the double-bind, but what does this have to do with the animal's behaviour at rest and when away from its work? Well, the emotions aroused by the triggering situation will have alerted the body for action, causing all the pysical changes to occur within it which have already been described. The muscles will be tense, the heart beating fast, the rate of breathing increased, etc.

Unless the body does something to use up this energy, it will be uncomfortable. Not wanting to go forward or backward, right or left, the individual tends to indulge in a 'displacement activity' – that is to say, it just does something to let off steam and release tension; the act it chooses tends to be of a type which brought it comfort in its youth, such as feeding or grooming itself (or in the case of horses, perhaps, escaping by galloping away). It is common to see a cat, thwarted of its goal, sitting down and licking its fur; a dog may scratch itself; a child may put its thumb in its mouth, an adult scratch his head.

These occasional displacement acts would not be considered neurotic; but if the act becomes a compulsive, regular feature of the individual's behaviour, which is repeated over and over again even in the absence of situations arousing the emotional stress, then it becomes a neurotic symptom – or, as it is known in horses, a vice. It is usually in a stable, where the animal cannot get rid of its tension in any other way, that this repetitive displacement act is most likely to be performed.

Heredity, it has been pointed out, plays an important part in determining the type of situation which an individual finds stressful. This is because heredity largely determines the needs of the individual as well as the sensory apparatus with which these needs can be satisfied. Heredity may also play a part in determining the actual act – the vice – which is adopted in displacement. It is known by those who breed horses that the offspring of a mare that crib-bites may become a crib-biter but seldom becomes a weaver, whereas the offspring of a weaving mare seldom becomes a crib-biter. If, as has been suggested, the habits of the mature neurotic are related to those which gave comfort in youth, one would suspect that the crib-biter gained its satisfaction

31

from suckling (it had a great need for food!) while the weaver gained its from galloping away (its need for food was smaller than its need for escape).

Treating Vices

Two of the main purposes of studying the origins of such unwanted acts as vices are firstly so that we can avoid producing them and secondly so that, if they do occur, we can treat or cure them. Ways of avoiding them have been stressed all through this chapter; what about curing them? There are two rather different – even opposing – methods which may be successful: rest and retraining. The purpose of the rest cure is to allow the individual to overcome its anxiety and generally to relax. During this time it is encouraged to eat as much as possible, put on weight and make up its depleted store of energy-producing substances. While this is happening, the general sense of security and happiness is reinforced by ensuring that everything in the environment is regular and simple so that the animal always knows exactly what to expect at any moment. It is provided with reassuring companions which will provide emotional support. These companions need not be of its own species. Even non-living comforters, such as a cuddly toy in the case of a human child or a piece of soft cloth in the case of a monkey can be a very great comfort to an overwrought animal.

The other method of treating the habit, that of retraining, may be started after a period of rest like the one outlined above, or it may be begun straight away, on the principle that it is just the behaviour which one is trying to alter not the basic emotional state. (In some cases, this last contention may be right. The basic emotional conflict which gave rise to the habit may have been cleared up a long time ago, but the habit has become so ingrained that it has persisted.) By punishing the individual every time the act is performed and rewarding it every time it is not, the individual can often be encouraged to establish new patterns of behaviour which are more desirable and less crippling than the old. (Sometimes the formation of new habits can be assisted if the animal is first put into a state of mental and physical exhaustion i.e. brain-washed.)

It is quite easy to see how this method can be successful in the treatment of vices in the working horse, and, indeed, variations of it are often used very successfully to cure rearing and napping, but there is a much greater problem to be confronted in trying to cure the stable vices. How are you going to punish a horse every time it wind-sucks or weaves? And how are you going to reward it every time it does not? And since the success of training depends on constant and inevitable reinforcement by reward or punishment, the treatment of the stable vices by retraining is seldom very effective.

Before beginning any form of positive treatment, of course, it is necessary to ensure that all possible causes of anxiety, and especially those which triggered off the original trouble, are removed. Here is another major snag; for although one can shield an individual from problems and conflicts for a certain length of time, when it is returned to its usual environment it will face the same sort of situation which led to anxiety in the first place. The individual which may have appeared to make a complete recovery while at rest, more often than not reverts to all its ruminations and rituals when returned to its original environment. The horse which stopped napping when it felt secure will revert to the habit as soon as it feels threatened. This is another argument in favour of retraining rather than resting. Advocates of retraining argue that this method will give the individual the strength to overcome any new difficulties it may meet, having overcome the old. Its success in these new situations will, however, still depend on its receiving rewards and punishments at the appropriate times; it will still depend on the presence of a firm, constant master.

In all this talk of vices, and especially in stressing their hereditary natures, the impression may have been given that a horse which produces a vice is a weak, inferior sort of animal which would be totally undesirable. However, it is possible for any horse to develop a vice if it is subjected to enough stress, just as any person could have a mental breakdown if he was subject to sufficient pressure in the sort of situation he personally finds painful. In the second place, the fact that an individual finds one situation stressful and anxiety-provoking does not necessarily mean that he is unable to cope with others. The very opposite is the case. The person or animal which is particularly well-equipped to deal with one type of problem is usually hopeless at others. If a horse shows an unpleasant stable vice (or if it rears or naps on occasions) this should not be taken as proof that the horse is totally valueless. It may well be a particularly brilliant performer, whose main anxiety is that it will not always do as well as it thinks it should.

This chapter has been written in the expectation that those who love and care for horses will be able to gain more pleasure from their equine companions if they know how their minds work. It is also hoped that a clearer understanding of horse psychology by the people looking after them will increase the happiness and contentment of the world's horses. Our knowledge to date only scratches the surface of all there is to be known about the mind. Scientific psychology is a rigorous discipline involving mathematics and a fairly long training, but psychologists do not have the monopoly on observation. Some of the observations made and reported by people who know their animals intimately even if they know little about any science, may be just as valuable as carefully controlled experiments; so every owner, rider, trainer, and groom can add to the knowledge of horse psychology if they take careful note of what they see and tell other people about it.

Ponies out at Grass

ELWYN HARTLEY EDWARDS

BELOW Wild horses. There are still vast areas in Europe and in Asia where horses roam wild in large numbers.

Ponies are well equipped to live outdoors throughout the year and unless they are to take part regularly in high-level competition this is a satisfactory method of keeping them, as well as being the most convenient for the pony owner. There are ponies that will not do well if expected to live out during the winter. Usually these are the finer type of near-Thoroughbred or ponies closely related to the Arab, but any of the British native breeds as well as those carrying a high proportion of native blood are frequently much healthier and more contented living out than when stabled.

For a pony living out is also a more natural way of life, although the domestic condition in no way resembles the true feral state. Ponies living in the wild, their survival governed only by the inexorable laws of nature, were self-reliant enough, but in the domestic state they are really extraordinarily helpless and entirely dependent for their well-being on the attention given to them by their owners.

In the wild, the herds of ponies had access to virtually unlimited areas of grazing which afforded grasses and herbs in great variety. In this environment, apart from the need to avoid the carnivores which preyed upon them and, at certain times of the year, the need to reproduce their kind, the principal preoccupation was the continual search for food. The herds therefore moved slowly from one grazing ground to the next, only rarely

expending energy by galloping at play or when fleeing from real or imagined dangers. In the spring and summer, when the weather was warm and feed plentiful and nutritious, the herds grew fat. Conversely, in the winter months, when the weather was severe and food scarce, the animals lost condition and physical energy. This was a natural cycle in which only the fittest survived.

The domestic environment of the pony is very different. Not only is he confined within a small area which, unless carefully managed, will rapidly become 'horse-sick' and cease to provide herbage in sufficient variety and quantity but he is, in addition, required to expend considerable energy working, often at speed and always when carrying weight. In consequence, the working domestic pony requires additional food, over and above that obtainable from his paddock, if he is to be kept fit for the purposes for which he is used.

Furthermore, by placing the pony in what is, in comparison with his natural state, an 'artificial' environment, he is subject to ailments which are the direct result of domestication. If, therefore, he is kept healthy and in good condition it is necessary for his owners to have sufficient knowledge of his needs and be prepared to devote considerable time and effort to ensure his well-being.

Paddocks and Fields

Obviously, the basic requirement is the possession of a suitable paddock or the availability of a similar piece of ground within easy reach of the owner's home. Much, of course, depends upon the size of the paddock and the interpretation of the word 'suitable'. Ideally, two–three acres per head, if properly managed, which implies amongst other things the resting of the land at intervals, are an adequate area but it is not by any means impossible to keep a pony on less.

To be 'suitable' a paddock should (a) provide as much quality herbage as its size allows; (b) be securely and safely fenced; (c) be free

ABOVE Healthy-looking wild Welsh ponies. The fact that wild ponies can look after themselves does not mean that a domestic pony, which is confined and working regularly can be neglected.

BELOW Horses in the Camargue, France. Many of these are in very poor condition although some are caught by the local farmers and put to work.

from poisonous plants or any foreign bodies likely to cause injury; (d) afford some form of shelter; and (e) have a proper supply of fresh water.

The question of the quality and quantity of grass grown is obviously of importance. The more natural feed that can be grown, the less will be the need to provide additional feedstuffs and vice versa, although, of course, the size of the paddock also has some bearing. Very small paddocks, of an acre or less, cannot, in fact, be regarded as anything more than places in which the pony can exercise himself and their value as a food source must be considered as minimal.

It is also an unfortunate fact of life that he who has the most grass will find it easier to manage properly and effectively, whilst he who has only a small area will find the fruitful management of it correspondingly difficult.

None the less, anything but the poorest sort of pasture can be improved. A prime consideration is drainage, which is no great problem on chalky, sandy or gravel-based soils but may be a considerable one where clay soils are concerned. The top-soil in these conditions will quickly become waterlogged because of the non-absorbent sub-soil; there is also practically no aeration possible in the latter. Plant life cannot thrive in these circumstances and will not do so until the land is drained effectively. The best solution, in many cases, is to use pipe-drainage but quite a lot can be done by keeping the ditches clean and open.

Most pastures in which horses are kept suffer from deficiencies of substances which are necessary for abundant plant life, namely lime, phosphates and potash. The only way to determine what deficiencies exist is to have the soil analysed. This can normally be arranged through the Country Agricultural Officer who will also be able to advise on the treatment necessary and on the best methods of fertilizing. A visual inspection of the land will usually give some indication of its deficiencies. A good quality sward consists of a great variety of leafy grasses mixed with some clovers and there will be a marked absence of weeds. Where the grass is matted or full of thick feg, mare's tail or sorrel the soil is acid and in need of lime, as is the case where there is a preponderance of buttercups and surface moss. An absence of clovers indicates phosphate deficiency. Sandy soils are particularly susceptible to deficiencies of potash.

Very poor pasture may be so far gone as to need ploughing up and re-seeding but any moderate sward will be improved by fertilizing and there are numerous proprietary chemicals which will clear persistant growths of nettles and other weeds. On a more basic level pasture can be kept more productive by employing a system of rotational grazing,

dividing the field into strips, however small, so that the grass is rested, perhaps fertilized, and given a chance to grow.

On small areas it is particularly essential to remove droppings regularly. The droppings encourage growths of coarse grass which horses, the most selective of grazers, will not eat. If droppings are not removed the field, within a matter of weeks, will be spotted with these inedible growths and the grazing restricted to the spaces in between them. An even more important reason to remove droppings is to control the worms, which are the particular scourge of the domestic horse kept on restricted areas.

All domestic horses harbour internal parasites which in general use pasture as the main vehicle in their life cycle. Much can be done to combat severe infestations by rotational grazing and the regular removal of droppings but in the main the principal attack must be concentrated on the host animal. The various types of worm found in equines and the methods employed to control them are described in more detail at the end of this chapter.

In order to keep the pony within the paddock adequate fencing is necessary. Good, thick hedges will do the job very well but in their absence other forms of enclosure must be used. The best fencing is undoubtedly that made from stout posts and rails and it is probably the safest, but it is expensive.

Far cheaper and almost as good is plain, heavy gauge wire stretched tightly between wooden posts. Care, however, should be taken to see that the lowest strand is not less than a foot from the ground otherwise there is the danger of a pony getting a foot caught. Barbed wire and chicken mesh fencing are not suitable and can cause serious injury.

All wooden posts should be treated with creosote which not only acts as a preservative but discourages the habit of wood-chewing. Trees within reach of ponies can also be treated in this way. To some ponies the bark is irresistible and if they once get the taste of it the tree will soon be killed off. It is often held

ABOVE Shetland ponies. These are a very old breed of small pony and are remarkably tough for their size. They are difficult to train as they are too small for any but the lightest adults and too strong for children.

that ponies chew wood because of mineral deficiencies in their diet. It may, indeed, be so and for that reason it is a good plan to equip a paddock with a mineral lick or, if it is obtainable, a lump of old-fashioned rock salt. Gates on fields in which ponies are kept need to be fastened with pony-proof fittings and should swing open easily. Coping with a heavy gate that has to be lifted one-handed whilst the other hand attempts to control an impatient pony is not very sensible and can cause accidents.

Most hedgerows contain their quota of poisonous plants, shrubs and trees. The most common are yew, which is also the most deadly, laburnum, ivy, deadly nightshade, hemlock, briony and so on. Ragwort grows around ditches and on scrub land. It is easily recognizable by its yellow flower and, in common with all the others, should be removed *before* a pony is put into a field where it grows.

An even more common source of injury is the varied debris of the twentieth century – the discarded tins, broken bottles, sharp pieces of metal, stray lengths of barbed wire and the ubiquitous plastic container. Ponies in small fields are the most accident prone of animals and for this reason should be inspected at least once daily for injury. All dangerous objects must, of course, be removed.

Nature provides ponies with thick, virtually waterproof coats against the worst of the winter weather but even with such protection they need shelter from cold winds and in summer somewhere to go away from the flies. Clumps of trees and high hedges provide such shelter but in their absence it is necessary to erect a simple, open-fronted shed with its back to the prevailing winds.

Finally, water is as essential to the pony's life as solid food, in fact more so. His body consists of 80 per cent water and whilst he can live

BELOW Strong serviceable fencing. Posts and rails are, however, expensive and do not provide any shade, as do hedges.

without any food at all for as much as 30 days he cannot survive for much more than a quarter of that time without water. How much water he drinks in a day depends on the temperature and the circumstances. At grass, in wet weather, he may not need more than six gallons a day but in summer he will easily consume twice that amount. Water must, therefore, be readily available in quantity and it must be clean. It is best supplied by a field pipe to a trough with rounded edges that cannot be knocked over but can be easily enough cleaned out. A heavy, galvanized tank can be pressed into service and fed by means of a hose but it is more difficult to keep clean. In summer scum must be cleared daily from the surface of the water and no trough should be placed where it can become a catchment for the autumn leaves. Stagnant ponds are filled with dirty water and are not suitable sources of supply.

The Pony in Summer

Given that a suitable paddock is available as a basis in the management of the pony, the owner must then be concerned with the animal's day to day care, which will depend in certain respects on the work required. During the spring and summer grass grows and is at its most nutritious state. A good pasture, containing grasses and clovers in variety, will, if it is big enough, provide sufficient food for a pony doing no work at all or doing a modicum of light, slow work. But whilst grass provides a balanced diet sufficient for a pony in its natural state it is a soft food producing a correspondingly soft condition and not supplying the energy necessary for work. If, therefore, a pony is to be ridden every day and galloped, jumped or put into gymkhanas each weekend grass alone will not be enough. In fact, too much grass will undoubtedly detract

Ponies grow thick coats in winter, but they still need some shelter and extra feeding They should not be over groomed as the natural grease in their coats affords protection.

DO NOT FEED

from his performance since it will make him too fat. Ponies in these circumstances will require more energy-giving foods and it will probably be advisable to restrict their intake of grass either by shutting them up in their shelter for most of the day, where they will be away from the flies, or confining them to a small area of the field.

Foods which are regarded as the principal sources of energy are oats, barley, maize, peas and beans; to a lesser extent pony cubes or nuts may be included in this category although they are in themselves a balanced diet. Oats, however, are as intoxicating to ponies as whisky is to men and can induce similar irresponsible behaviour. Bigger ponies, ridden by older and more experienced children, can be fed on oats but for smaller ponies used by younger children they are better left out of the diet. Maize is heating but indigestible and peas and beans produce such exuberance and have such heating properties that they are best reserved for horses doing a great deal of work. Barley, on the other hand, is a good food if fed carefully and all ponies will do well on cubes without becoming silly.

Just how much food a pony requires is not easy to state since it depends very much on the individual and the type and amount of work he does. Some ponies need only a pound or two of concentrate food for them to be on their toes, others seem to need a considerable quantity to put them into the right frame of mind and to bring them to the required physical condition.

As a guide, however, a 13hh. pony working for an hour or two each day and competing at weekends with an enthusiastic rider would need a ration of *at least* three to four pounds of nuts per day mixed with one pound of bran and fed damp with the addition of some sliced carrots or an apple. If this were not felt to be sufficient then an additional half pound per day of *bruised* barley could be given. Barley should not be fed whole as it is then very indigestible.

On very sparse grazing it might be possible to turn the pony out for the whole 24 hours, dividing the concentrate feed into two and giving one early in the morning at least an hour before the pony is ridden, and the other at the end of the day. Where the total concentrate feed exceeds four pounds it is, indeed, always advisable to divide it into two.

On lush grazing it is absolutely necessary, if the pony is not to become fat, to bring him in for most of the day and to feed the concentrates as before. In fact, whilst grass is a natural food for ponies, too much of it is not good for them, whether they are in work or not.

Most ponies are either of the native breeds or closely related to them. The original environment of these ponies was the wilder mountains and moorlands of Britain where vegetation is sparse in the extreme. As a result the ponies learnt to exist on the minimum of food to convert what they did get most efficiently. Quantities of lush grass are not needed by such animals and whilst they will

eat it voraciously, barely taking time to breathe, it does not suit their metabolism and it can have dangerous effects. Ponies that are allowed to get over-fat in summer are less able to work effectively, put more strain on their legs and internal organs and can contract a particularly painful disease of the feet called laminitis. In essence, laminitis is an acute inflammation within the inner foot affecting the sensitive laminae. Since the outer wall of the foot cannot expand the condition is very painful and causes severe lameness and distress.

Following severe attacks, almost always affecting the forefeet, the pony may well suffer recurrent onsets of the disease and will in any case become restricted in his action.

Ponies at grass during the summer are also susceptible to skin ailments and can, even in the best run establishments, pick up lice. The solution in this instance is to dress the animal thoroughly with a good anti-parasite powder. More common ailments are *humour*, a pimply condition of the skin caused by overheated blood and over-eating; *itchy mane and tail*, which can be produced by a parasite or, most frequently, by overheating of the blood; and the distressing allergy *sweet itch*, which it is thought is caused by some constituent in the summer grass combined with the rays of the sun.

Humour is best treated by adding a daily handful of Epsom salts (about four oz.) to a bucket of water and giving the dose as a regular thing.

Itchy manes and tails are less likely to arise if the areas are kept free of scurf and dirt. The affected parts can be washed in a medicated shampoo and coconut oil rubbed in gently will alleviate the condition.

Sweet itch, a severe irritation in the areas of the mane, neck, withers and dock, is intensely painful and is often accompanied by a yellow discharge and loss of hair. The only solution is to keep the pony off the grass and out of the sun and get the vet. to prescribe a course of treatment.

Care of a Pony's Feet

Since most ponies are ridden on roads and other hard going, shoeing is necessary to prevent the foot becoming sore or breaking away. Since ponies walk, trot, canter and gallop on their feet, the greatest attention has to be given to shoeing. A properly fitted shoe on a well-shaped foot is the best means of combating the various foot troubles that occur. Bad shoeing and neglected feet that are allowed to grow too long upset the pony's action and can place unnecessary strains on ligaments and joints.

BELOW New Forest pony.

RIGHT As soon as the grass starts to grow in spring or early summer Thoroughbred mares and their foals can go out to the fields, even before the foals are weaned.

Feet in bad condition can also give rise to diseases within the foot. It is, therefore, very well worth while to find a really good farrier, even if it means a long journey to his forge, and to have regular attention to the pony's feet.

The horn of the foot, like our nails, grows all the time and may, indeed, grow as much as a quarter of an inch in a month. Shoes should, therefore, be removed every four weeks or so, whether they are worn out or not, and the foot rasped to its proper shape. The pony's feet should be inspected daily to check the 'clenches' (the ends of the nails which are turned over the horn). Clenches can 'rise' and when they do it is possible for the pony to injure himself by striking a foot against the opposite leg.

Ponies not in work and kept out without shoes should have their feet dressed and rasped into shape every five to six weeks, otherwise the foot grows too long and breaks away. If the foot is brittle and liable to break it is probably better to fit 'tips' on the toes.

Grooming

In summer the pony loses his winter coat and can be groomed thoroughly so that the coat and skin are kept clean. Grooming, also, of course, improves the pony's appearance and stimulates the circulation.

A full grooming kit consists of the following: Dandy brush – a stiff whisk brush used, primarily, on the legs to remove mud. Usually it is too prickly to be used on the body but when the coat is coming out it is often the most effective tool to use. It should not, strictly speaking, be used on the mane and tail since it breaks and pulls out the hairs. Body brush – a soft bristle brush used on the body and for brushing out the mane and tail. Water brush – a soft, boat-shaped brush used damp to lay the mane and tail which can also be used to put

Here the blacksmith is fitting the shoe to the pony's foot. The clouds of steam look alarming but rarely worry the horses. Farriers are very skilled and sometimes fit the shoes while the metal is still hot, as an exact fit is important. Generally speaking all horses and ponies should have shoes fitted, except when they are turned out to grass together for any length of time and then it is wise to remove the hind shoes so that they do not kick each other. Metal tips can be fitted instead.

on a final shine. Curry comb – a metal comb of toothed blades having a wooden handle. It is *not* used to clean the pony but to clean the body brush. Sponges – for cleaning eyes, nose and dock. Stable rubber – a linen cloth used as a pad to give a final polish. Mane comb – a small metal comb used for trimming the mane, tail and leg hair. Hoof pick – the best type to use is a good large one, not the fiddly folding type. A piece of brightly coloured string tied to the ring will often prevent it from being lost in straw, etc. Rubber curry comb – this is an excellent aid which *can* be used on the body and is very effective in removing the coat.

When you groom the pony it is best to begin high up behind the ears and work backwards with the body brush. The secret of good grooming is to stand well away from the pony so as to be able to get the whole weight behind the brush. The body brush should be used rhythmically in the right hand whilst the curry comb is held in the left. Every three or four strokes the brush should be cleaned briskly on the comb. When brushing the head be particularly careful that the wooden edge of the brush does not bang against the bones of the face. Similar care must be exercised when brushing the loins. In this area the brush must not be banged down hard lest it should cause damage to the kidneys which are situated relatively close to the surface.

Eyes and nose should be wiped with one sponge, a separate one being used for the dock. Clean the legs with the dandy brush, but again be careful not to knock the pony with the edge of the brush. Brush out the mane and tail with the body brush and then lay them with the damp water brush. Thick manes and tails can be pulled to give a neater appearance, but pulling has to be spread over some three weeks otherwise there is a danger of making the parts sore and the pony, in consequence, irritable and unco-operative. Pulling is a skilled job which is best learned from an experienced horseman.

To pull the mane, brush it over to the wrong side and then take about half a dozen hairs in the mane comb, push the comb up to the roots and pull sharply. The mane will then be pulled from its under-side and short hairs will not stand up like those of a shaving brush along the crest. When sufficient hair has been removed the mane can be cut to a length of about five inches – but not with a pair of scissors otherwise it will look horrid. Use a sharp penknife between fingers and thumb.

Before pulling the tail wash it well in a good shampoo and when it is dry brush it out. Remove the surplus hairs one by one, pulling out no more than a dozen a day. Each day damp the tail and put on a tail bandage to keep it in shape but don't leave the bandage on for more than an hour or two otherwise the continued pressure will break the hairs. There are various ways in which the tail can be shaped but the nicest one is to pull the top and leave the bottom fairly full. The bottom of the tail can then be 'banged', i.e. cut to the required

length. To 'bang' the tail get someone to hold it up at the dock, which is how it will be carried in movement. Calculate a hand's breadth below the hock and with a pair of large scissors, such as are used for paper-hanging, cut the hair off in a straight line inclining the scissors slightly upwards from rear to front. The tail will then finish in a straight line when it is held up as the pony moves. To give the pony a final shine use a damp stable rubber in a pad all over the body.

The feet have to be cleaned out, a job that can either be done first or last. Clean out each foot with a hoofpick using the pick from heel to toe along the side of the frog. If the feet are very dirty they can be washed out using an old brush but too much washing is to be avoided as it will remove the natural oils secreted from the coronary band. Hoof oil can then be applied to each foot to improve its appearance and to help the natural oiling process.

Grooming the forelock with a body brush and the tail with a curry comb – the body brush would be more suitable for the tail so as to avoid splitting the hairs.

Pony coats in summer frequently become dusty and scurfy and there is no harm in shampooing the pony thoroughly if, for instance, he is to compete at a show. Use a good, medicated shampoo and choose a warm day. The pony must be dried off thoroughly, particular attention being paid to the heels which if left wet can become chapped.

Winter Care

In winter the pony grows a thick coat and a film of waterproofing grease is formed on the skin. Ponies kept out should not therefore be groomed, an exercise which would clearly reduce the effectiveness of the protective coat. The most that need be done is to brush off the surface mud before riding.

Grass in the winter months does not grow and what there is will be of little nutrient value. It follows, therefore, that if the pony is to be maintained in good condition, regular supplementary feeding will have to be carried out. The fact that in cold weather a large proportion of the food intake will be used to maintain body temperature is yet another reason why ponies need generous feeding through the winter, whether in work or not.

In addition to the concentrate ration already mentioned for a working pony, at least ten pounds of hay per day should be fed. Hay should be given in two feeds, morning and evening, with the bulk being reserved for the last one. To save waste, feed the hay in a net, making sure that it is tied up sufficiently high so that the pony, if he paws at the net, cannot get a foot caught.

At present, hay is expensive and scarce so it may be necessary to economize by feeding a mixture of hay and oat straw in the ratio of seven pounds of hay to three pounds of straw. Oat straw is not so nutritious as good hay but a sample of good quality is probably a lot better than a similar quantity of poor hay. It is, in fact, possible to feed oat straw alone if hay is not available but it would then be wise to increase the ration to 12 pounds. Further economies can be made by feeding sugar beet pulp or nuts, which are excellent conditioners. In both cases, however, the sugar beet must be soaked overnight and then fed at the rate of about three pounds soaked weight.

The available food will be put to better use if a mineral block, such as Keep, is placed in the field. These blocks not only contain vital minerals, etc., but stimulate the digestive system into breaking down and employing the food intake more effectively.

Ponies kept at grass cannot for obvious reasons be clipped and the presence of the coat will therefore place limitations on their use. The heavy coat causes excessive sweating during work of a strenuous nature and, in consequence, a loss of condition would occur if the pony were worked fast and hard regularly. There is, however, no reason why children should not hunt their unclipped ponies during the holidays, so long as the ponies are receiving an

adequate concentrate ration. Every effort should, however, be made to bring the pony home cool and dry. Rain, will not do the pony much harm and when turned out he will probably have a buck and a kick and a roll in the muddiest part of the field. On return from hunting there is no reason why the pony should not be given a warm bran mash, whilst he is being inspected for scratches and cuts, before being turned out. His hay should be ready for him and later he can be given his normal feed.

Older children, intending to hunt regularly through the season, may feel the need to have a clipped pony. In these cases, however, whatever the clip employed, whether a 'trace' or a 'hunter' clip, the pony cannot be expected to live out entirely and will have to be brought in at night and turned out during the day in a New Zealand rug. This is a perfectly satisfactory arrangement but although the pony will exercise himself, it makes for more time and labour.

Ponies remain remarkably healthy during the winter and very rarely get colds. It is, in fact, more likely that the ones brought in at night will catch colds than those kept out for the full 24 hours. They are, however, subject to minor ailments such as *thrush, mud fever* and *cracked heels. Thrush* can be caused by dirty conditions under foot. Usually it is found in stabled horses but it can affect ponies kept in small, muddy paddocks. The complaint is rather like the human one of 'athlete's foot'.

The frog sweats and emits an unpleasant smell and there may also be a discharge from the cleft. Feet should therefore be regularly inspected and, at the first sign of thrush, washed out with a strong disinfectant and then packed with Stockholm tar.

Mud fever is a skin irritation affecting the lower legs and sometimes the belly. It is more prevalent in certain areas than in others and it can cause acute lameness necessitating veterinary attention. Prevention is better than cure and the risk of ponies contracting the complaint can be much reduced, if not removed, by smearing the lower legs with vaseline or with an antiseptic ointment like Protocon.

Cracked heels can be caused by excessively wet conditions. The heel becomes chapped and it becomes painful for the pony to move. As with mud fever, applications of vaseline will prevent the complaint.

Worms

All horses and ponies carry a worm burden to varying degrees, the worms, as we have noted, using pasture as a principal vehicle in their life cycle. There are three common worms, the white worm, whip or seat worms, and the red worm, which is the most dangerous of all. In addition, during the summer, ponies can suffer from stomach bots, which are not true worms and which are ingested, without doing much harm.

BELOW Horses and ponies love to roll after they have been ridden as their skin is often itchy while they are drying off.

RIGHT Company is very important for horses and ponies.

Mare and foal in a paddock.

The white worm is the most common. It can be up to a foot long and as thick as a pencil and is easily seen in the droppings. In large numbers it will cause severe loss of condition and in bad cases can result in a stoppage or even a rupture of the gut.

The worm lays its eggs in the gut and they are passed out with the droppings. They then hatch on the pasture and re-enter the animal with the grass he eats, which is one very good reason for removing droppings regularly. The small worms then enter the gut, penetrate the

intestinal wall and move through the internal organs until the process begins again.

Whip or seat worms are about a couple of inches long and very thin. They occur only in the rectum and are not harmful to the general condition but do cause intense irritation around the anus, causing the pony to rub continually.

Red worm develops in the same way as the white worm but is infinitely more dangerous. They feed on blood and in sufficient numbers can cause stoppages in the blood stream. The result of a heavy infestation is loss of condition, listlessness, a stary coat, anaemia and diarrhoea. The droppings smell strongly, the stomach distends and the skin appears to be stretched tight. In neglected cases the worm may penetrate and close a main artery, cutting the blood supply to the bowel, whereupon death will almost inevitably occur.

Control of the worms can, however, be effected by regular dosing under veterinary supervision. *Adult horses and ponies need worming at least twice a year and more if necessary.* Youngstock, with less resistance to the worms, need more frequent treatment. A veterinary surgeon, before prescribing, will take samples of the droppings to determine the degree of infestation. Doses are made up in pellet or powder form and are given with the food.

The importance of worm control cannot be over-emphasized. Regular treatment throughout the animal's life is vital and ponies newly bought, whether appearing to be suffering from worms or not, should be dosed as a matter of course.

Tetanus

This is a fatal disease caused by the entry of the tetanus bacillus into the body through a wound or scratch. Horses and ponies can, however, be immunised against the disease by a course of injections of anti-tetanus serum. Obviously it is a precaution well worth taking.

Teeth

Finally, once a year teeth should be inspected by a vet. They can become worn and sharp or be broken and cause difficulties in mastication.

Summary

If I had to summarise the principles involved in keeping ponies at grass a few words would be sufficient: 'knowledge intelligently applied and constant supervision'.

In summer and winter ponies should be visited once, and preferably twice, each day. These visits give the owner the opportunity of inspecting the paddock, checking water supplies, fencing, etc., and examining the pony for any sort of injury or for signs that all is not well. In general, ponies are tough and healthy, but they can become ill or lame.

The state of health is revealed through the appearance of various parts of the body, the excreta and by means of temperature, pulse and respiration. Dull, staring coats indicate worms or malnutrition, as does a tight skin. Redness instead of a healthy pink colour in the membranes of eyes and nostrils indicates inflammation. White colouring in these areas is caused by debility, yellow by liver disorders, whilst purple may be caused by pneumonia.

Limbs should be examined daily and should feel cool and free from swelling. Droppings, or the appearance of them, are a good guide to condition. In health they are well-formed, slightly moist and do not smell strongly. In summer, of course, the new grass may cause

loose motions, which is natural enough, but any strong smell or coating of mucus gives cause for suspicion and action.

I have tried to cover as many important subjects about looking after ponies as is possible within the limitations of space and, indeed, the restrictions of the written word. The best way to learn about animals is at first hand from experienced owners and there comes a point when this is essential. However, beware of ignorant but confident owners and remember the principles as outlined here.

ABOVE A pure bred Arab foal.

Stable
Management

ELWYN HARTLEY EDWARDS

THE EFFIE BISHOP B

Horses are kept stabled so that they can more easily be conditioned for the work they are to do. Hunters, for instance, if they do no work in the summer months, will be put out to grass in late April–early May and brought up in early September, remaining stabled through the hunting season. Event horses and jumpers will probably be stabled through the summer months, when they are competing, and perhaps put out for a rest, being stabled at night, towards the end of the year.

It would not be possible, for the reasons given in the last chapter, to compete consistently at the highest level with a horse kept at grass. It is, none the less, important that stabled horses should at some time during the year be allowed out to grass where they can relax and unwind both physically and mentally. The basis of management in the case of the grass-kept pony is the paddock. In the case of the stabled horse it is the box in which he spends the greater part of the 24 hours.

Since one of the prime objectives in caring for the stabled horse is to keep him relaxed, interested and content, the box should be as near to the ideal as possible. Its position is important. It is better, for instance, for it to be sited facing south, out of the head winds which would make the horse's life uncomfortable, and where it receives as much sun as we are likely to get in our climate. If it can also face a yard where the horse can see and take an interest

Well built loose boxes round a yard. The doors are a good height and fitted with two bolts, while the window opens correctly so that the air goes up and then circulates around the stable without creating draughts.

in what is going on around him, so much the better. Horses, like children, need to have their minds occupied and the comings and goings of dogs, humans and even chickens will prevent them from becoming bored.

Whatever the type of stabling used, three factors are essential in the construction. The box must be *well ventilated*, *well drained* and *well insulated*. In the first instance ample ventilation is needed without any draughts, which are just as bad for horses as for humans. Draughts cause aches and pains and are the surest means of giving the horse chills and colds.

If the top door is left open and the box is sufficiently high there will rarely be a problem. Louvres, however, set high in the rear wall will help to clear upward rising bad air which may accumulate. Windows, placed next to the doorway, should open inwards from the bottom hinge so that air enters in an upward direction

and is not directed downwards on to the horse.

Shutting top doors, even in bad weather, is not to be recommended. The box can fill with fumes and become fuggy, which will cause the horse's coat to shine but will also give him colds. In cold weather the door should be left open, an extra rug put on the horse and the ration of heating foods increased to compensate for the extra used by the horse to keep himself warm. Horses cannot have enough fresh air – the more they get the healthier they will be.

Drainage is most effective when it is simple. Old-fashioned stables, beautifully built, were frequently spoilt by the drain being set in the centre of the floor, which was often constructed of lovely Staffordshire blue bricks. Such drains, not surprisingly, frequently became blocked and the box, as a result, was filled with unpleasant smells. One would hardly think of putting an open drain in one's sitting room and there seems no reason why the horse should be expected to put up with one in his.

The best form of drainage is to have a ridged concrete floor sloping slightly towards the doorway and an open drain, which is easily swilled out, set on the outside of the door. If placed inside the door it makes it uncomfortable for the horse to stand and look out of his box.

Insulation is a matter of the materials used in the construction of the box. These should keep the building cool in hot weather and warm in cold. Brick built stables with cavity walls present no problems but the common type of wooden boxes require lining on the inside, a practice which will also strengthen the building against horses that get pleasure from kicking walls. Corrugated iron, sometimes used for roofing, is not a good insulator and it is better to use asbestos sheeting, but not, of course, for walls.

The size of the box, in the case of the wooden structures, is already predetermined by the manufacturer, but for a big horse it should certainly not be less than 12ft by 10ft with the eaves as high as possible to allow for free ventilation. The height of the door is generally about 4ft 6in, which allows the horse to look out without discomfort but is high enough to discourage thoughts of jumping over it. Should one have a horse with a marked propensity for jumping out of his stable, a sliding wooden bar fixed a foot or more above the door will usually prove to be a sufficient deterrent. The width of the door must not be less than 4ft otherwise it will be possible for the horse to knock his hips as he passes in and out, a seemingly minor accident but one that can cause a chipped bone or even a fracture.

Two bolts are necessary on nearly all stable doors, one of the usual type on top and a kick-over one at the bottom. This will ensure that bolt-openers, of which there are not a few, will have their efforts frustrated and the lower fastening also discourages the persistent door-banger who likes to hear the door rattle away each time he gives it a kick.

Stable Equipment

Certain fittings are necessary within the stable, notably rings for tying up haynets and one for tying up the horse if that should be necessary. A manger will also be required for feeding and is usually of the triangular shape, made either of galvanized metal or plastic, which can be dropped into a wooden frame built at breast height across the corner of the box.

Alternatively the horse can be fed in a round feed tin from the floor. Both types are easily removed for cleaning. Self-filling water bowls, involving the installation of a permanent water system, are time savers but otherwise water can be given from buckets. Hay is best fed from nets rather than from the old type of wall-fitted hayrack, which causes the horse to imitate a giraffe when feeding and ensures that all the dust and seeds fall into his eyes.

Electric light switches should be placed outside the box out of harm's way and lights

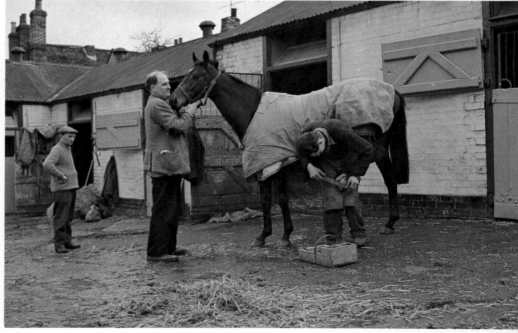

within the box fitted out of the horse's reach and covered, as an extra precaution, with wire mesh. Obviously, stable tools – forks, skips, barrows, brooms, etc. – need to be in good order and it is usually more economical to buy only the best.

Bedding

A good bed is necessary for the horse's comfort. Poor, thin beds discourage lying down and may contribute to injuries caused from contact with the hard floor. Whatever form of bedding is used it should provide a dry, warm and resilient bed which is at the same time absorbent and deodorizing.

Straw is the most common form of bedding but gone are the days of long wheat straw. Now it is all short, combine stuff. Wheat straw, however, is the most resilient form of bedding and is not palatable to horses. Oat straw flattens more easily and is a positive invitation to bed-eating. Barley straw is prickly stuff but the combine variety makes a good enough bed. The advantage of straw, in all cases, is that the box cleanings are saleable, which is not the case with other materials.

Sawdust can be used for beds, but requires much attention. Sawdust from 'green', rather than seasoned woods ferments easily and becomes hot when wet and packed hard. Wet patches and droppings have to be removed quickly and the bed forked and turned daily. Wood shavings, which are less likely to ferment, make better beds but this material is not absorbent. Peat moss is possibly the most efficient deodorizer of all and is also very absorbent, but it requires as much frequent and regular attention as sawdust. The advantage of bedding material other than straw is that it will not be eaten by the horse; its disadvantage lies in the difficulties of disposal. Soaked patches left in the box can cause rotting of the feet and can 'scald' those parts of the body with which it comes into contact. Straw beds need to be cleaned out each day and the box brushed out with disinfectant before the bed is replaced. Soiled straw and droppings go to the muck-heap and the stuff that is only slightly damp can be dried out and used again. For the sake of the horse's health muck-heaps should not be placed too close to the stable. On the other hand, for the sake of the groom, they should not be too far away. Neither, for the sake of wooden buildings, should they be sited against a convenient wall. The ammonia fumes given off will ruin wood with which they are in close contact. Effective sites for holding manure can be made on a patch of concrete enclosed on three sides with railway sleepers or with more expensive concrete block walls.

In either case manure needs to be well packed down and the edges of the heap kept tidy. Decomposition is accelerated in a well-packed heap and the resultant increase in heat produced will discourage fly breeding. Arrangements should, of course, be made for the regular removal of the heap.

A Lipizzaner mare at the Lipizza stud where these horses are bred in Yugoslavia. The usual tether in a stall is a chain from the head collar which goes through a ring on the wall and has a weight at the other end. This is to avoid any possibility of the horse becoming tangled up and at the same time gives him certain freedom of movement.

Clipping Horses

Horses that are stabled in winter have their coats removed by clipping for good reasons. A thick, protective coat is necessary to the horse living out and is no hindrance to him unless he is asked to work fast. To the stabled horse, however, where the object is to maintain the animal in hard and fit condition, the coat is a drawback that will cause him to sweat excessively at work and as a result lose condition. It acts, indeed, like a sweat suit. Without a heavy coat the horse can work without distress and therefore more efficiently, and it is easier for him to be kept clean. Additionally, a clipped horse can be more quickly dried off than one wearing the equivalent of a heavy fur coat.

The winter coat starts to grow in September and needs to be 'set', or established, before clipping, which is usually done in early October. By Christmas the horse will need a second clip. The type of clip employed depends on the type of horse and the work he does, but is, also, very much a matter of preference.

A 'full' clip removes the whole coat. A 'hunter' clip leaves a saddle patch on the back and all four legs unclipped. The height to which the unclipped hair is left can be gauged by measuring, on the hindlegs, a stretched hand's breadth from the hock upwards to obtain the line at the rear, and a similar hand's breadth from the stifle downwards to obtain a leading edge. On the forelegs the line is

RIGHT Clipping a ten-year-old Irish Cob in a special clipping box. This should only be done by an expert and there should also always be two people since if the horse is startled the blades may well cut him.

determined by measuring one outstretched hand from the elbow down and two from the knee upwards.

A 'blanket' clip leaves a patch generally approximating in size to the area covered by a galloping sheet, thus giving protection to the whole back and particularly the loins, and the legs again are left untouched. A 'trace' clip is when the hair is clipped from belly and flanks and usually up the under side of the neck as well. It is usually, but by no means always, reserved for hunting ponies kept out during the day in New Zealand rugs and also, as the name implies, for harness horses.

The arguments put forward in favour of the 'hunter' clip are (1) that the saddle patch will prevent galls and 'scalding' of the back and (2) that the hair left on the legs gives protection against thorns, cuts, cracked heels and chills.

Conversely, it could be argued that whilst a fine-skinned horse would benefit from having the saddle patch left on, a horse with a heavy coat would be encouraged to sweat excessively under the saddle and could as a result develop a sore back. A thick saddle patch is also more difficult to dry.

In the end it all probably depends on the type of horse. Fine-coated Thoroughbreds are in most cases better off 'hunter' clipped whilst their more plebian country cousins will be easier to manage if clipped right out. A sensible compromise in the latter case would be to give a 'hunter' clip but to use coarse leg-blades,

which do not cut so close, on the horse's legs. Clipping is a matter of practice and is made easier by the possession of a well-maintained electric clipper, sharp blades and strict adherence to the manufacturer's instructions.

Thereafter the prime requirement is a clean and dry horse. No clipper will cope with a thick, scurfy and matted coat. If the weather is not cold and the horse well rinsed and dried there is no reason why he should not be shampooed a few days before it is intended to clip. Once the horse is accustomed to the noise of the machine clipping can begin on the shoulder against the lay of the coat, since this is the least sensitive area.

Manes and tails, unless the former is to be hogged (i.e. all the mane removed), should not be touched with the clippers or they will resemble shaving brushes. The dock area on the quarters can be clipped in a V shape – a straight line across the top of the tail looks most odd.

The belly and the parts between the hindlegs are ticklish and it is best when these areas are reached to have an assistant to hold up a foreleg by the toe between finger and thumb. In theory the horse cannot then move any of the other three feet. In practice, it is as well, when clearing out between the hindlegs to grasp the tail some two-thirds of the way down. A pull on the tail at the right moment will cause the horse to put his weight on to the leg nearest the operator and thus prevent any kicking.

It is not necessary to clip the mane at the

A black Akhal-Teké rolling in sand. This is a special rolling place which is part of the superb equipment at the Akhal-Teké stud in Ashkhabad in Russia.

withers nor to cut out a piece behind the ears for the bridle head if the mane has been neatly pulled. Where there are wrinkles in the skin, as there are under the elbows for example, the skin has to be stretched flat and pulled with the hand. The hair inside the ears should not be cleaned out as it forms a natural protection against wind and rain. It is sufficient to run the clipper along the edges, holding them together so that both are trimmed in one action. Horses easily become cold, and as a result start to fidget when being clipped, unless a rug is put over their backs as soon as it is feasible to do so.

When the horse has been clipped the skin surface will be covered with grease and dirt, however clean he seemed at the beginning. This grease can be removed by making the horse sweat. It is done by putting on as much clothing as is available and giving the horse a short period of sharp exercise. The horse will sweat when the rugs are taken off and the grease can be removed by strapping the animal vigorously with a damp wisp.

Rugs and Stable Clothing

Having removed the horse's protective coat it is necessary to make compensation by providing sufficient clothing to keep him warm. The basic needs of the stabled horse in this respect are a thick underblanket, a lined jute or sail cloth top rug and probably a cellular anti-sweat sheet which will act as a very efficient insulator for the body. There are, however, modern variations on the conventional clothing, notably a brushed nylon lined rug made on the anorak principle which, it is claimed, can be used without any other blankets. A set of wool bandages is also necessary to keep the legs extremities warm.

Top rugs are secured either by an integral surcingle, as in the case of the nylon rug, or by a body roller of web or leather. The latter is frequently made with a hinged metal top-arch which adjusts the pads automatically to the shape of the back and acts, also, as an anti-casting device, since the hooped arch prevents

the horse from rolling over on to his back.

Stable clothing unless well fitted can cause chafing at the breast and also on the withers and the back. In the two former instances chafing can be prevented by padding the rug in these areas with either sheepskin or foam. Back injuries are caused by ill fitting rollers or in the case of both rollers or attached surcingles by excessively tight adjustment.

The condition and fitness of the stabled horse, apart from the provision of comfortable and otherwise suitable housing and an adequate supply of clothing, depend upon the management of his feeding, grooming and exercise. The object is to produce a strong, muscle-fit horse, capable of performing his work without ever being exerted to the limits of his strength and endurance, while remaining relaxed and calm in his mind.

Feeding in balance and in the proportions relative to the work done and in accordance with the natural digestive system will supply the means to build up the body and the material to make muscle, as well as producing the energy necessary for work. Grooming keeps the horse healthy and clean and stimulates the skin, whilst wisping improves circulation and promotes the growth and tone of muscle. Exercise removes surplus fat, develops and strengthens muscle and provides an essential interest for the horse.

Feeding

To provide balance the diet must include six constituent elements: proteins, fats, starches and sugar, water, fibrous roughage, salts and vitamins, all of which are largely interdependent. Proteins replace muscular wastage, form body tissue and produce energy and heat. Fats, starches, etc., produce heat and energy. Water is essential since without it the natural processes of the body and the digestive system cannot function. Fibrous roughage is the agency by which concentrate foods are broken up and absorbed. The precise function of salts and vitamins is not entirely clear but it is known that they are necessary to the organism and if deficient in the diet general health is severely affected.

The foods containing these constituents can be divided into bulk, energy and auxiliary foods.

Bulk foods are represented by hay and chaff (a mixture of chopped hay and oat straw) and by the various brands of cubes, etc., which in themselves constitute a balanced diet. Hay, for the stabled horse, provides the main source of fibrous roughage and can contain high percentages of proteins.

Energy foods for practical purposes can be regarded as oats, barley, peas and beans and maize.

Auxiliary foods include bran, containing a high proportion of salts; linseed, a fattening food, and green foods such as carrots and other roots. Additionally there are many feed-additives on the market which are of value. The quality of food today is lower than in the

BELOW Feeding time away from home. The hay net is well tied at a height where the horse cannot get his foot caught in it. Nets avoid wastage and unlike racks prevent the seeds falling in the horse's eyes. This chestnut has a hunter clip which has almost grown out and the horse behind is trace clipped.

RIGHT A beautiful chestnut dozing in the sun. A chain such as this across the door should only be used when the horse is under supervision – for instance when the stable is being cleaned out.

BELOW RIGHT Three Haflingers just turned out to grass in early spring after spending the winter in stables. Notice the space of this field and the shade the horses will have in summer from the trees.

past and these feed-additives can do much to remove deficiencies.

The quantity of food required depends on the individual horse but as a general guide the total daily intake for horses between 15–16hh. is 24–26lb and for animals over 16hh. 26–28lb. The proportion of bulk to energy and auxiliary food is also dependent upon the horse's make-up and on the work he is doing.

For a horse exercised daily (an essential element in the management of the stabled horse) and hunting one day per week the proportion would be 50 per cent bulk to a corresponding amount of concentrates. Horses in fast and harder work would require an increase in concentrates but the proportions of bulk feed in the diet cannot be below one-third of the total intake or the concentrates cannot be broken up and absorbed by the digestive system.

The manner in which the total intake is fed is entirely governed by the horse's digestive apparatus and his small stomach. The limited capacity of the latter and the inability of the system to cope with large quantities of concentrate food at one time gives rise to the golden rule, *feed little and often*. Hay, the prime digestive aid, may be given in larger quantities because it is eaten more slowly, the bulk of the ration usually being reserved for the night when the horse has more time in which to eat and digest it. Concentrates, however, have to be given in smaller quantities, not more than four–five pounds in any one feed.

The daily programme has then to be arranged so that the horse is never worked immediately after feeding, the second golden rule. This has to do with the position of the stomach, which is behind the diaphragm. The diaphragm is in contact with the lungs in front and the stomach behind. Thus, after feeding, when the stomach and bowels are distended, the former will press against the diaphragm.

If the horse is worked in this condition the expansion of the lungs caused by the exercise

will result in pressure on the diaphragm which, in turn, presses on the stomach. The effect is not only to impair the breathing but also to interfere with the digestive processes taking place in the stomach and bowels. This will cause indigestion and possibly severe colic. At worst, if the work were fast and prolonged, the lungs could become filled with blood and a rupture of the stomach occur. Water must, of course, be freely available to the horse at all times. In the case of a horse receiving a total ration of 28lb per day of which 14lb is hay, the remaining 14lb of concentrates will have to be given in no fewer than three feeds and preferably four. Where a horse is in hard work receiving say, 10–12lb of hay and the remainder

in concentrates, the number of feeds will have to be increased to as many as five.

How much energy food in the way of corn has to be fed is governed by the amount and type of work done as well as the effect it has upon the horse. If a horse is too full of himself the answer is either to cut the corn back until he is more manageable or to increase the exercise period. The essential rule to be observed is that the intake of energy foods should equal, or ideally be a shade under, the output of energy occasioned by exercise and work.

In the case of the horse receiving 14lb of concentrates plus the same amount of hay as a daily ration, the concentrates might comprise, in the simplest form, 10lb oats, 2lb bran and 2lb made up of roots, soaked sugar beet nuts, perhaps a few nuts, molasses and a mineral additive, the whole being fed in three or four feeds. One would expect such a horse to be having between 1 and $1\frac{1}{2}$ hours exercise each day and at least 45 minutes to one hour would be spent grooming him. The programme of the day, which has to be strictly adhered to as any upset in routine upsets and worries horses, might then be as follows:

7 am	First feed; adjust clothing; pick up droppings.
8.30 to 10.30 am	Exercise after quartering (i.e. a quick grooming of the horse).
10.30 am to 12 pm	Mucking out; small feed hay (4lb); grooming; pick up droppings.
12.30 pm	Second feed; pick up droppings.
4.00 pm	Third feed; pick up droppings.
6.30 to 7.00 pm approx.	Wisping; small feed hay (2lb); pick up droppings.
7.30 pm	Fourth feed; pick up droppings.
10.00 pm	Last haynet (8lb); pick up droppings.

This horse would be a high quality animal used to working regularly and accurately.

After a period of severe exertion, a day's hunting for instance, the horse requires an easily digested meal on his return to the stable. He should be given a warmed drink, perhaps containing a bottle of stout, or a thin linseed gruel and then fed a warm linseed mash. Rest days, probably the day after hunting, are an opportunity to feed the weekly bran mash which will keep the horse's bowels in order.

The full food ration of the stabled horse must, of course, be approached gradually in the same way that exercise must start with long periods of walking until the horse has been made fit

A Swiss-bred mare and her two-day-old foal. Already the foal has to become accustomed to wearing a foaling slip – this should be well oiled and very carefully fitted at regular intervals as he grows.

enough to work at faster paces. Just as the physical structure of the horse would be in danger of breaking down if subjected to violent exercise when the animal was fat from grass, so the internal system would be strained if suddenly expected to deal with large quantities of concentrates.

In the present economic climate there is a temptation to buy the cheapest foods available without considering their quality. This is a false economy. Poor food is less nutritious pound for pound than feedstuffs of the best possible quality and may, moreover, cause digestional upsets. It is, however, no use buying good and expensive food unless it is stored where rats and mice cannot get to it.

Tainted food is as unacceptable to the horse as to humans, and if it should be eaten, will cause illness. Nor is it economical to feed good food if the horse has (a) not been wormed or (b) not had his teeth attended to. In the first place the food is used by the worms, and in the second a great deal will be wasted on the floor of the box because of the horse's inability to chew.

Grooming

The stabled horse, living in 'artificial' conditions and consuming large quantities of concentrate foods, has an increased quantity of waste matter for disposal. Much of the waste is got rid of through the increased breathing rate of the lungs and by excrement but almost

A Show hack in peak condition which has been achieved through careful feeding, grooming and exercise. The diamond pattern on his quarters has been brushed on specially for showing. Show hacks can be crosses between Anglo-Arabs and small Thoroughbreds and are usually very highly trained and good mannered.

as great a proportion is dispersed through the skin, which must, therefore, be clean if it is to function effectively in this respect.

Grooming, already described in the previous chapter, is best carried out *after* exercise when the horse is warm and the pores open, but wisping, or strapping, is better left to the evening. The reason is that wisping encourages circulation, which naturally slows down during the night hours. The purpose of wisping is to develop and harden muscle and to stimulate the skin and the circulation. It also produces a 'bloom' on the coat caused by the release of the oil from the glands surrounding each hair.

A wisp is a tightly woven rope of hay, about eight feet long, which is wound into a pad. The wisp is used damp and brought down energetically on the horse following the lay of the coat. It is used on the quarters, shoulders and neck but not upon the head, loins, belly or legs.

Exercise

The stabled horse must be exercised, whatever the weather, each day except for the rest day, when he should be walked out and allowed a nibble of grass. Exercise, apart from its obvious benefits, keeps the horse alert and interested but it will not do this unless it is varied and carried out intelligently. Trotting the same route every day only results in boredom.

On exercise days, as always, the horse must be brought home cool and dry; if he is not then he must be walked until he has dried off lest he catch a chill. When wet it is better to trot the horse home so as to bring him back warm, but not steaming! He must then be rubbed down with straw, an anti-sweat rug put on and this, in turn, covered with a jute rug on inside out so that the lining is not made wet. In the absence of a sweat sheet handfuls of straw on the back, covered with a rug, will serve.

RIGHT Horses in head collars much too big for them enjoying a splash in the water.

OPPOSITE PAGE ABOVE Wild horses are always on the move. A fit, stabled horse must have adequate exercise which should consist of two hours riding a day and two hours in the paddock.

OPPOSITE PAGE BELOW A Thoroughbred yearling out on a frosty morning. If it is really cold horses can be turned out rugged.

After severe exercise, such as hunting, the horse should be brought in dry and cool. The saddle, on which the girth has already been loosened, and the bridle can then be removed. After a drink sweat marks on the back and girth can be sponged away and the parts dried. Then the rug is thrown over him whilst the head and throat are sponged and dried, the ears being 'stripped', i.e. hand rubbed to promote circulation. The areas between the hindlegs, under the tail, the sheath and round the elbows have to be attended to with the sponge and then the legs can be inspected for cuts, thorns, etc.

If the mud is dried on the legs it can be brushed off quickly and the limbs given a quick hand rubbing upward towards the heart. When the dryness of the heels has been checked the legs can be bandaged.

Finally the horse should be given a brisk going over with the body brush, the mud rubbed off his belly, by hand if necessary, and his clothing put on. The object is to make the horse comfortable quickly so that he can rest and have his food.

An hour or so after the horse has been given a linseed mash he should be looked at to see whether he has eaten up and has not 'broken out', i.e. started to sweat again. Should he have broken out he must be dried off once more. The ears are given a last rub and then the horse can be given his haynet. He must be visited again before being left for the night to ensure that he is warm, comfortable and settled.

LEFT Alison Dawes schooling one of her horses.

BELOW LEFT A classically elegant rider sitting side saddle on an English-bred hack. They are performing a well balanced trot full of impulsion for the camera.

BELOW David Broome exercising a young horse. The horse is wearing a numnah under the saddle. This gives extra protection and support to a horse starting work at the beginning of the season.

In circumstances in which the horse finishes hot and sweating, as he would after the speed and endurance phase of a three-day event, he can be sponged down with warm water, then dried by hand and by being walked about. To avoid a chill an anti-sweat sheet should be put on the horse under a light rug. Without a top covering the sweat sheet is of no use since it is only when it is covered with another that it can act as an insulator.

Following severe physical exercise the body is in a weakened condition and its functions are correspondingly less efficient. It is essential at these times that the body temperature and the rate of circulation are maintained and that the digestive system is not overloaded with food.

The final rule to be observed in the management of the stabled horse is that of cleanliness in all things. Beds must be clean and droppings removed frequently through the day. Likewise feed bowls and mangers have to be spotless, while water buckets must be filled with clean, fresh water, not just topped up. Of course, the horse himself must be clean.

An old groom's tale (and there are just as many of those as there are old wives' tales) is that about allowing cobwebs to collect round the stable as fly-catchers. With no respect at all this is nonsense – an insecticide spray is far more effective if flies prove troublesome. One suspects this more stupid of the horsey maxims to be the product of lazy horse-masters. We do not tolerate cobwebs in our houses, so why should the horse in his?

BELOW A Welsh Cob wearing a show bridle for an in-hand class. Native or Arab breeds are always shown with the forelock left free and not plaited. The lead on the bridle is passing through the bit ring on the near side and is attached to the ring on the far side – this stops the horse turning its head towards the leader.

Family Sport

ELIZABETH JOHNSON

Clubs and Classes

When you have chosen and bought your horse or pony you will want to make the maximum use of it and there are endless opportunities for all classes of horse and rider. If you are keeping the horse at home, give it time to settle in to strange surroundings and don't invite all your friends to come and 'have a go' the moment it arrives. With a few lessons from a local reputable riding school, a lot can be learnt which can then be put into practice at home on your own horse. What frequently happens is that having acquired his first horse or pony, the owner abandons the regular riding lessons, believing himself to be a complete expert simply because he is the proud owner of his own horse and no longer reliant on the riding school hacks. How wrong that is. One never stops learning in the world of riding, and one of the best plans is to go with your new horse or pony to have lessons together. These lessons will assist enormously with the problems that are bound to face a new partnership and, even if you are experienced, another pair of eyes will be a good idea.

If the animal is to be shared among a family new to horse ownership, it would be a good opportunity for the whole family to go along to the school and listen to the advice given. Where a riding school is not convenient, much help and knowledge can be obtained by joining the local Riding Club or Pony Club branch.

Pony Clubs and Riding Clubs

In many parts of the world pony clubs provide a wealth of pleasure and education for the young people who belong to them. In Britain, the Pony Club was founded in 1929 when a branch of the British Institute of the Horse was turned into an organization to create enthusiasm for riding amongst children, and to teach them how to ride and care for their animals correctly. The project was almost immediately successful, and by the mid1930s there were more than 8,000 members.

The Second World War put an end to pony clubbing, however, and it was with some misgivings, considering the great interest in things mechanical, that the Pony Club

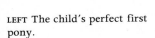

LEFT The child's perfect first pony.

RIGHT A confident combination at a gymkhana. The pony is well under control and is not disturbed by the fact that his rider is about to wave a red flag under his nose. This couple must have practised at home since the pony knows what is expected of him and is enjoying the class. The excitement of the show will unsettle a pony that has not been well taught beforehand.

horse and if we do it often enough he will very sensibly cease to obey because of the discomfort which follows.

Having prepared the foal, the actual fitting of the foal slip can be made. This will require the employment of a little innocent guile – a quality to be encouraged in all trainers of horses.

If the trainer is very skilled, the fitting of the slip can be accomplished single-handed, but in the majority of cases the presence of an assistant will make the job easier and lessen the risk of the foal damaging itself by some violent reaction.

The role of the assistant is to control the foal's quarters, which will be done by the usual encircling arm. So positioned the assistant will be able to prevent the foal from rearing up in fright, and possibly coming over backwards, by urging the foal forward or by pushing the quarters to one side.

The trainer stands at the foal's near-side shoulder, holding the slip with a hand on each cheek-piece. He or she then passes the nose-piece over the foal's muzzle and brings it quietly upwards into place. All that remains to be done then is to pass the headstrap behind the ears and fasten it up to the appropriate buckle. It sounds very easy but more often than not the foal will be frightened by the unaccustomed pressure on its head and react accordingly by trying to run backwards. If this happens then the assistant must counter the movement by pushing the foal forward, and therefore *into* the head slip.

Once the slip is in place the foal can be persuaded to move forward for a few strides by the trainer giving the command 'walk-on' and exerting a gentle pressure on the lead strap, whilst the assistant reinforces the order by pushing the quarters forward. Once the foal has grown used to the feel of the slip he can be led to and from the paddock alongside his dam.

Obviously, the leather of the slip must be made soft and supple by repeated applications of oil or grease well before it is put on the foal, otherwise it will chafe and cause discomfort which may lead to a quite unnecessary rebellion.

It is of the greatest importance at this stage that the foal is taught to lead from both sides. A fundamental objective in training is to encourage equal suppleness on either side of the spine, an essential requirement for the later training under saddle. Far too frequently young horses, and even mature horses, are 'one-sided', i.e. they find difficulty in turning with equal facility in both directions. Usually, horses turn more easily to the left than the right, a situation which is brought about for two reasons. First, there is a natural tendency from birth for the spine to be slightly curved and secondly, because this curvature is further confirmed and established by consistently leading the young animal from the near, or left side. Habitually led in this fashion the horse carries himself virtually bent round his trainer's hand. In consequence a block of

muscle is developed on the right side of the body with no corresponding development on the near-side. It then becomes a matter of difficulty to bend the body to the right and we have the classic 'one-sided' horse. Teaching the young foal to lead from both sides will go a long way towards obviating this problem and will save much time and effort later in his training.

Constant handling of the foal is just as necessary and gradually it should be possible to pick up each foot while the foal stands quietly. Foals that have learnt the lesson of having their feet picked up regularly will rarely be any trouble when they have to be shod later in their lives. Grooming with a soft brush as a sequel to initial hand rubbing should also be introduced as part of the foal training.

These lessons take place in surroundings which are familiar to the youngster but at some point he has to learn something of the world outside his stable and paddock. An ideal introduction is to enter the mare and foal at one or two local shows, a proceeding which will involve him in being loaded into a trailer or horse-box and having some lessons in the behaviour expected of him in the show ring. He has, for instance, to be taught to be run out independently in-hand and to allow the mare to do likewise without being too much of a nuisance.

Obviously, these lessons have to be practised at home well before the date of the show and the same is true in the case of trailer drill.

Although the foal will almost always follow its dam it is not advisable to put the mare into the trailer first in the hope that the foal will follow. It is quite probable that the foal will remain rooted to the spot at the sight of the relatively dark container into which his mother has disappeared. The mare, separated from her offspring, is then likely to panic and attempt to rush out of the trailer and, at once, the foal has been set a bad example. It is more sensible and less risky to lead the foal first, cradling it between the arms of two people and propelling it into the box. The mare, anxious not to be separated from her baby, will then enter without more ado.

These very elementary lessons early in the foal's life contribute very largely to his future training. If they are learned well they represent a sound foundation for the following stages. If they are not, and the foal is frightened or confused, the effect will be made evident later and from the outset the trainer's difficulties will be increased.

A young foal must, of course, be treated gently but he should not at any time be allowed to become 'cheeky'. Normal high spirits are excusable but nipping, kicking or standing on end to box his leader with the forefeet are to be discouraged firmly by the use of the voice and by a sharp smack delivered at the appropriate place.

Training can certainly not be neglected but it should not occupy a disproportionate amount of time. The foal should be allowed the liberty

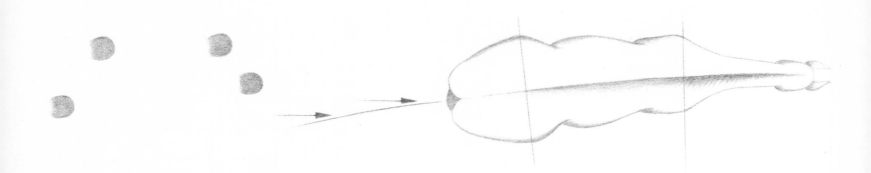

Straightness. The horse on the
left is moving incorrectly.
The hind feet are not following
in the track of the fore-feet.
The horse on the right is
moving in a straight line.

of an ample acreage in which he can develop
naturally with companions of his own age and,
most importantly, he requires adequate
supplementary feeding to ensure his full growth
potential. As a general guide a foal should
receive 450g (one pound) of concentrate food
for each month of his age up to a maximum of
2.2–2.7kg (5–6 pounds) according to his size.
The feeds are given daily and should consist of
nuts or cubes, bran, oats, linseed, apples,
carrots etc, and should also include powdered
milk and a ration of cod-liver oil to promote
bone formation. From September until the
spring young horses will also require ample
rations of soft meadow hay.

At the age of two years the horse should be
in receipt of a daily ration of up to 3.2kg (7
pounds) concentrates and by three years, when
his primary training begins, he should be eating
4.1kg (9 pounds) of food per day divided into
three feeds. Thus prepared he should be ready
for the more serious training of the second
stage to begin.

Stage 2 Primary Training

The second stage of training begins in the
horse's third year and in Europe it is usual to
bring the horse up from grass in early April
and to work him lightly through the summer
months to August or September, after which
he can be rested until the following April when
he is in his fourth year.

Once more it is advisable to define the
objectives to be achieved if the training is to
have a clear purpose.

Recognizing that the three-year-old is as yet
undeveloped in mind and body, the aims in the
second stage are as follows:
1) To accustom the horse further in the
acceptance of discipline and to being handled
to a much greater degree than previously.
2) To prepare the horse physically to carry
weight.
3) To teach him to *accept* weight on his back.
4) Having achieved his acceptance of weight to
teach him *how* to carry it, which will involve
his making adjustments to his natural balance.
5) To teach the rudiments of control by the
rider.

These overall objectives will be achieved
gradually by dividing the training into distinct
phases, each having its own objectives, but all
the work and the methods employed will also
be directed at producing a state of CALM in the
pupil. Without CALM it will be impossible to

attain the desirable triumvirate pronounced by
General L'Hotte, one of the greatest of the
French masters, as containing the essential
principles of training. L'Hotte summed up the
essentials in the three words, CALM,
FORWARD, STRAIGHT. Calm is a state of
mind, and is not to be confused with lethargy.
Once it is achieved in the horse he can then be
taught to go FORWARD, a quality which
implies not only immediate and willing
obedience to the legs aid, but also a positive
mental attitude. True forward movement is, in
fact, a physical manifestation of a mental
attitude.

For a horse to be STRAIGHT means that his
hind feet follow exactly the track made by the
fore-feet, the full propulsive effort of the
hind-legs being delivered directly to the front
and the effect of their thrust is not lost by
being directed to one side or another and away
from the direction of the movement.
Straightness is achieved by the equal
development of muscle on either side of the
horse and the correction of the congenital
curvature which has already been mentioned.

It is easy enough to appreciate the necessity
for calm, but it is perhaps not so easy to
understand the remaining requirements. To go
forward, instinctively, is, however, an essential
in the riding horse and when it is not present
the rider is at the mercy of his horse and loses
control. An obvious example of disobedience
caused by the horse ceasing to go forward is the
refusal to jump a fence which is within his
capacity. He then disobeys the indications of
the rider's legs. Very simply he stops because
he ceases to go forward. The need for a horse
to be straight is even less recognized. Clearly,
the mechanical efficiency of the structure is
improved by a horse tracking up correctly
without any deviation of the hind-legs but
there is rather more to it than that. Straightness
in the horse certainly involves equal physical
development on either side of the spine etc.
but it also involves the ability of the rider to
position the quarters, which are the origin of
directional movement, by the use of his legs.
Straightness, in part, is achieved by inducing
mobility in the quarters so that they can be
moved from side to side by the action of the
rider's right or left leg. It must follow that if
the rider is thus able to control the shift of his
horse's quarters he will not only be able to
impose straightness on his horse but will be
able to prevent any unwanted movement which

would result in a change of direction and a consequent loss of straightness. Given that a horse is confirmed in forward movement and is straight he must be under control and the chances of his refusing (by ceasing to go forward) or running out at a fence (because he has shifted his quarters to enable him to make an unwanted change of direction) must be reduced to a virtual minimum and, theoretically indeed, rendered impossible.

Early in April the young horse is stabled and made familiar with the routine of the yard. Many trainers advocate the young horse being allowed a 'free' period at liberty during a part of the day so as to allow him to stretch his legs, get rid of his high spirits and generally relax. This is a good practice and prevents boredom, and the usual antecedent of this frame of mind – mischief-making.

Circumstances may not permit an ideal routine to be carried out in its entirety but what is important is what goes on in the time devoted to grooming, exercise and stable training.

Grooming has the practical effect of cleaning the horse and contributes to his health and well-being, but it also provides an opportunity for a relationship to be established between trainer and pupil. Properly carried out it can help, too, in the formation and development of muscle. Initially it has to be done gently but by gradual stages it can become more thorough. Particular attention has to be given in these first weeks to the handling of the feet, the head and the mouth. The feet will, indeed, need trimming by the farrier during this period and if the horse has been properly prepared there is no reason why this first experience with the smith should be other than peaceful.

The handling of the head is important as a preparation for bridling the young horse, while teaching the horse to allow his mouth to be opened and inspected serves a two-fold purpose. In the first place it will make the eventual introduction of a bit that much easier and secondly it will give the trainer the opportunity of seeing the state of his pupil's teeth, which at this time and up to the age of six are in the process of being shed and repalced by permanent ones. There is nothing to be done about the teeth but a regular inspection will reveal inflammation of the gums which may cause temporary discomfort and will provide an explanation for an occasional display of fractious behaviour.

Ideally, a horse should stand quietly untied when being groomed and handled but initially he has to be taught to tie-up and, in any case, there will be frequent occasions when he has to be tied. This is perhaps the first lesson in stable training and it can be accomplished, as can most things, by firmness and patience – strong-arm methods are neither necessary nor, in the long run, helpful. All that is necessary is a fairly long lead rope attached to the headcollar and passing back through the wall ring to the trainer's hand. Holding the rope the trainer grooms the horse with his free hand. If the horse steps back the rope is allowed to slip through the ring, after which the horse is urged forward again and once more a light tension is taken up on the rope. If the practice is repeated on a dozen or more occasions the horse will have learned how to stand still and the rope can be tied in the usual way without any fear of his running back.

An equally important lesson is for the horse to learn to 'move over' in his box in response to a request to do so. It can be taught by just bending the horse's head towards one and then tapping the flank with a stick whilst at the same time giving the verbal command. Gradually one can move further back towards the hip and tap and command as before. In quite a short time one should be able to stand in line with the dock and achieve the same result with no more than a pat and a word.

The secret lies in the correct positioning of the body in relation to the horse's body so that he cannot misunderstand what is wanted.

Exercise in the first few weeks is undemanding and consists of nothing more than the horse being led about the place from a lungeing cavesson and being allowed to observe the normal activities that are taking place. To start with an assistant can be employed to follow behind and encourage the horse to walk freely forward. As in his foal days the horse will be taught to lead from both sides and then, towards the end of the first three or four weeks, he will be expected to walk properly in-hand. Walking in-hand is an important exercise since it forms the basis of forward movement and is a preparation for work on the lunge. The trainer teaches the lessons standing at the shoulder, holding a long whip behind his back in his free hand. He gives the command 'walk-on' and at the same time taps the horse with the whip to ensure that he steps off smartly. Quite quickly the horse will learn to move forward on the verbal command alone and he can also be taught to halt and even to trot at the spoken word.

Once the work in-hand has advanced sufficiently it is time to begin the important exercises on the lunge line, in which the horse circles the trainer to either hand. In the stable, grooming can be extended to include wisping (thumping the muscles of the neck, shoulders and quarters to assist toning and development) and, by placing the horse against a wall, he can, by a discreet pressure on the nose and a spoken command, be taught to take a few steps backwards in preparation for the ultimate rein-back under saddle, which is yet a long way in the future.

Lungeing is possibly the most important and useful of the conditioning exercises and its purposes are worth examining in some detail.

Physically, its objects are:

1) To promote the build-up of muscles without their being formed in opposition to the rider's weight. To develop the muscles equally on either side of the body.

2) To make the horse supple laterally by the equal stretching of the dorsal, neck and abdominal muscles on either side.

3) To induce a tension in the spine by the encouragement of a rounded outline brought about by an extended carriage of head and neck accompanied by an engagement of the hindlegs under the body. The latter will always be easier on the circle since the inside leg is bound to be more actively engaged and placed further under the body.

4) To encourage an increased flexion of the joints as the result of greater and more supple muscular development.

5) To encourage the flexion of the spine, as far as this is possible, with the object of correcting the natural curvature.

6) To improve the balance – an object best achieved on the circle because of the need for greater engagement of the hocks.

Mentally, the exercise has just as much importance. It inculcates calm and accustoms the horse to the habit of discipline, teaching him obedience to the first of the aids, the voice. Finally, it teaches the horse to GO FORWARD.

Lungeing is, however, a demanding exercise for the young horse and initially the periods spent on the lunge should not exceed 10–15 minutes. As the horse becomes stronger the lessons can be extended to as long as 30–40 minutes, the remaining part of the exercise and work period should be devoted to walking the horse to where he can see traffic etc.; leading him across country and generally getting him used to new sights and sounds.

As the lunge training progresses the horse will be fitted with a body roller, accustoming him to the pressure of a girth round his middle. Side-reins can in time be attached to this.

The next step is to have the horse shod to prevent him from becoming footsore. No trouble should be experienced but it will take a few days for the horse to grow used to the feel of shoes on his feet.

It is now necessary to introduce the bit to the horse's mouth, to assist the improvement of the carriage by the use of side-reins on the lunge, to fit a saddle, and then to put a rider on the horse's back, a proceeding which is known as 'backing'. To accomplish all of these things will take some weeks, depending upon the aptitude of the pupil and his development.

The bit is at first worn suspended from the lunge cavesson which, on the first occasion that it is fitted, is fastened by a strap from the offside. The bit, together with the bribe of a few sliced carrots is then held in the palm of the hand and gently inserted into the mouth, the near-side bit ring being finally attached to the ring on the cavesson which is there for the purpose. The horse wears the bit for an hour or so each day and may even be given a small feed while it is in position. This will encourage him to 'mouth' the bit, relaxing his jaw and making saliva. He will also wear the bit while working on the lunge so that he learns to accept its presence without showing resentment.

The type of bit used depends very much on the preference of the trainer. Some trainers prefer the 'mouthing' bit fitted with keys, which are supposed to encourage the horse to play with the bit and so relax his jaw, others will use the plain half-moon snaffle either of rubber, which is very mild, or of nylon.

Side-reins, or the use of them, are always a point of controversy, but essentially they are used to 'bring the horse together' and are shortened progressively to this end. At first side-reins will be attached from the roller to the cavesson rings and only when the horse is used to them will they be attached to the bit itself.

Lungeing with side-reins attached to the bit teaches the horse to accept the presence of the latter but it does not, of course, teach the horse about the varying bit pressures that will be employed by the rider, nor how he is expected to respond to them. The ground for teaching the ridden hand aids can, however, be prepared in the stable. The trainer will often start by standing in front of the horse, holding a bit ring in either hand and vibrating the bit slightly upwards and to the rear. The horse responds by momentary relaxations of the lower jaws and when that happens the pressure is released and the horse rewarded. Similar pressures on one bit ring will produce a dropping of the nose and a relaxation of the corresponding side of the jaw. The lessons can be taken further in the school where the horse can be persuaded to walk forward by an assistant while the trainer, a little in advance of the shoulder, holds a rein in either hand. A slight vibration on both reins accompanied by the command 'whoa' teaches the halt. The changes of direction are taught by the vibration of a single rein on the side towards which the turn is wanted.

Some authorities teach the rein-aids on long reins while the horse is driven from behind. Long-reining to be effective, however, requires an expert, well-skilled in the exercise.

ABOVE A horse on the lunge must keep a perfectly rounded circle with the horse bent uniformly from poll to tail. The trainer maintains a triangle of control of which he forms the apex, the rein and whip the sides, and the horse the base.

RIGHT A lungeing cavesson.

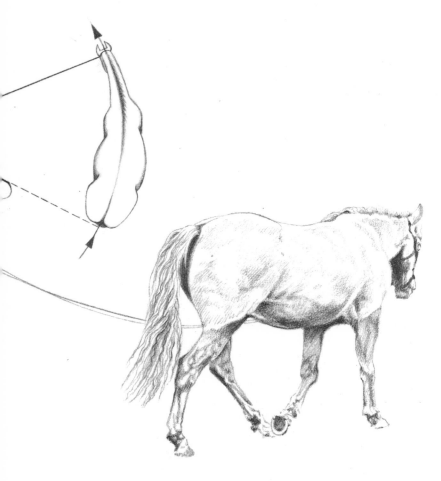

The fitting of the saddle is done when the horse is well-used to wearing a roller and many people will also take the precaution of placing a weighted sack over the horse's back each day before actually putting on the saddle. Prudence dictates that the first attempt will take place after the exercise period, in the stable, when the horse has rid himself of any itch in his heels.

When the horse works on the lunge calmly without showing any resentment towards the saddle on his back, the business of putting up a rider can begin. Once again the preparation for this event takes place in the stable after exercise. A lightweight, agile assistant is needed who will in the first instance do no more than put his or her weight across the horse's back, making no attempt actually to sit on the horse. If the horse, suitably distracted by a bowl of oats, accepts the weight calmly then, by degrees, a leg can be put over and the assistant is mounted. The schooling continues in the training area with the rider mounted and the horse circling the trainer on the lunge as before. At this point the rider makes no effort to control the horse at all. The object is to get the horse to accept the weight on his back.

The final phase in the three-year-old training is concerned with teaching the horse the elementary aids, to *carry* the weight on his back at walk, trot and canter and, additionally, to introduce the first lessons in jumping.

The exercise period, or periods, since it is quite reasonable to work the horse twice during the day, must now, perforce, be extended. The lungeing exercises continue and may include the strengthening and balancing exercises practiced over spaced poles on the ground and then over similarly spaced cavalletti. The ridden work will take place in the schooling area but the lessons learnt there will also have to be put into practice out in the countryside. A significant proportion of the exercise will, therefore, consist of hacking excursions around quiet lanes and in the countryside. Hacking the young horse about is a most important part of his education. It introduces him to a variety of new circumstances and is the best safeguard against boredom and a loss of interest in his work.

But, before he ventures out into the world outside of his familiar surroundings he must first be taught, for his own sake as well as for that of his rider, to obey the aids.

Once he is working quietly on the lunge with the rider in the saddle, the aids can be taught by the trainer reinforcing the physical action of the rider with his voice, to which the horse has already been made obedient. To teach the aids from halt into walk, for instance, the rider, having obtained the horse's attention by a squeeze of the legs and a slight closing of the fingers on the reins, applies both legs decisively behind the girth. As she does so the trainer gives the command 'walk-on' and, if necessary, sweeps the thong of his lungeing whip behind the horse to encourage further a movement forward. It will not be long before the horse associates the squeeze of the legs with the verbal command and moves forward from their action alone. So, increasingly, control passes from the trainer to the rider with the latter gradually assuming the major role. Once the aids for walk, trot and halt have been learned and the horse has been accustomed to the application of the rein aids on the circle, the lunge line can be removed and the horse ridden in the school under the rider's control.

How well the horse responds depends very much, of course, on the competence of the rider – the more accomplished the latter the better will be the result. At this point it is absolutely essential that the aids, often supplemented by the use of the voice, should be absolutely clear. If the horse is confused now there will be no chance of his learning the more advanced work in the secondary stage of training. For this reason the aids to turn should be quite unmistakeable and even exaggerated. The accepted turning aids on the schooled horse are made by applying the inside leg on the girth, to maintain the impulsion; the outside leg is held slightly to the rear of the girth, supporting the action of its opposite number and preventing an outward swing of the quarters; the fingers of the inside hand close to bend the head and neck in the direction of the movement and the outside hand is opened a little so as not to oppose the bend. Used in this way the rein is employed as that of *direct opposition,* i.e. it opposes or blocks the forward movement on the side to which it is applied, and in consequence the movement is re-channelled so that the quarters, when the right rein is used, must be pushed over to the left and vice-versa. But that is far too complicated an action for a young horse to understand, let alone obey. If it is used, the pressure on one side will only confuse him, restrict his stride and cause a loss of the essential forward progression – the very last thing that is wanted at this early stage. It is, therefore, more sensible to keep the horse moving forward and to make the turn by using a simple *direct* or *opening* rein effect. To use the rein in this way the rider carries the inside hand well out to the side, pointing the thumb in the direction that is to be taken. The action will pull the horse's nose over to the left or right, according to which rein is used, and the shoulders will be shifted in the required direction. The aid is exaggerated but its intention is quite unmistakeable to the horse and his forward movement is not interrupted.

So far the horse will have been ridden from his mouthing bit or from the half-moon snaffle. It is now an appropriate time to make a change to a jointed snaffle with a good fat mouthpiece. If a half-moon snaffle has been used it may not be necessary to replace it. Indeed, if the horse is going well and is happy in his mouth with this particular type of bit there is no reason to make a change just for the sake of doing so.

The school lessons will involve the execution of simple figures, changes of direction, elements of circles, transitions from one pace to another and so on. They can, however, include a little work over a grid of poles on the ground or low cavalletti – exercises which will have already been done on the lunge. This work will strengthen the quarters and hindlegs and help the horse to find balance under his rider's weight. They are, of course, also a very useful preliminary to jumping.

Increasingly, however, more emphasis will be placed on the hacking activity, since the ability to ride the horse outside of the school area is the ultimate goal. Ideally, a young horse should be ridden out initially in company with an older and more experienced companion from whom he can draw confidence and whose example he can follow.

On the roads the older horse can shield the young one from traffic by being ridden on his outside and a little ahead of him, and so long as he is steady, the youngster will soon lose any fear he may have felt about road vehicles.

Hacking, in fact, provides the greatest opportunity for schooling. Crossing undulating ground, for instance, compels the horse to make constant adjustments to his balance and short, fairly steep ascents and descents are excellent developers of muscle. It is also possible to introduce other little balancing exercises. On a good bridlepath, for instance, the horse can be asked by judicious use of hands and legs, to slow down and speed up the pace, which is the beginning of the exercises designed to make him supple longitudinally. Out in the open, preferably on a slight uphill slope, the trainer has the ideal place for teaching the horse to canter, a pace that is usually too difficult for a young horse to accomplish under saddle in the confined area of the school. The early efforts at canter will not be polished performances but the horse is learning how to carry weight at this pace and will improve continually.

Small ditches, low logs and little streams can all be used to advantage. Given a lead by an older horse the youngster soon learns how to negotiate these obstacles and the knowledge gained will stand him and his rider in good stead for the future.

Stages of the canter. The canter is a three-beat pace. This horse is leading with the right leg.

Towards the end of this primary stage it should be possible to make a change from the use of the simple direct turning rein to the more conventional rein of direct opposition.

Finally, the horse can be asked to do a little simple jumping, over very low fences, before his primary education is concluded and he is rested over the winter months. He will already have learned on the lunge and under saddle how to cross a grid of low cavalletti, but for his first jumping lessons it will be prudent to revert to the lunge. The first jump is very simply accomplished by a rearrangement of the basic cavalletti grid. The trotting distance between each cavalletto is between 1.2m (4ft) and 1.8m (6ft), depending upon the size of the horse and the length of his stride, and usually a grid consists of four cavalletti. To make a fence, the third cavalletto in the line is placed on top of the fourth, the height of the two being about 50cm (20in). The horse is then lunged over the grid in the usual way at trot and will, almost always, make no trouble about hopping over the last element. Jumping without the burden of the rider's weight is obviously easier and the horse can learn to judge his fence without interference. Once, however, he is jumping confidently and freely, the exercise can be repeated with a rider, although the lunge rein will be retained and the rider will not at first act with the bit rein. Thereafter, it should be possible to dispense with the lunge line.

Before he is rested for the winter, the horse's teeth should be examined and if necessary he should be wormed. The feed ration, of concentrates and hay, must be continued through the winter months if the horse is to be brought up in the following April in a strong condition ready for demanding work.

Stage 3 Secondary Training

There will be a pronounced difference in the physical appearance between the three and four-year-old horse. The latter should, if he has been well-fed and cared for, be big, well-grown and strong by the time he is brought up in the April following the completion of his primary education. Of the two, this secondary phase is likely to give rise to more problems than the elementary training, and not only because the work is more advanced. The young horse, more sure of himself now, may begin to assert himself and on occasions his natural exuberance may turn to outright disobedience.

It is, therefore, necessary to consolidate the work done in the previous year, insisting upon obedience in the exercises already learnt, before attempting to teach anything new.

As in the case of the primary training, the secondary stage of education will divide naturally into phases, the whole comprising a number of subsidiary objectives leading to the desirable end product of the all-round horse.

In general, within this stage, the following are the objectives that are to be attained:
1) Progressive physical conditioning.
2) The furtherance of the mental development.
3) The placing of the horse 'on the bit' and 'on the hand'. (That is, the horse moving forward in response to the action of the legs to take up contact with the bit and going as it were 'between the rider's legs and hands'.)
4) Increasing the lateral and longitudinal suppleness of the horse by gymnastic exercises. (In effect the aim is to produce a horse that can be likened to a spiral spring which can be compressed and extended at will and which is able to be bent laterally in either direction).

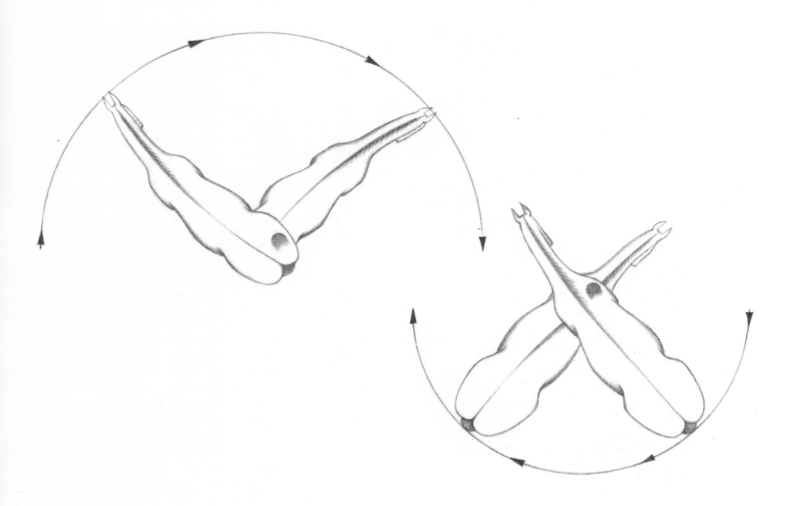

5) Teaching the aids up to the secondary standard.

6) Inducing by the use of school figures and exercises a greater degree of straightness in the horse.

7) Continuing and extending the jumping training.

8) Introducing greater exposure to road traffic.

9) Making the first introduction to the double bridle.

The conditioning of the horse is a gradual process obtained, as before, through feeding, grooming and exercising. In the secondary stage of training a four-year-old should be able by September to be doing some two and a half hours of exercise and work each day. Approximately 45 minutes each day, excluding the early morning quartering, should be spent on grooming and wisping, and the feed ration may have risen to as much as 4.5 to 5.5kg (10 to 12lb) of concentrates for a horse of 16hh. or so, and about 7 to 8kg (16 to 18lbs) of hay daily. Rations, like work, must of course be increased by gradual stages and no hard and fast rule can be made about exact quantities, since the requirements vary from individual to individual. Clearly there is no sense in putting up with an over-fresh horse unable to concentrate on his work. The solution in such a case is either to cut back the corn ration or increase the work, or, of course, to resort to a combination of both.

The remaining objectives will be achieved by the combination of work on the lunge, a method of training retained well into the schooling programme; ridden schooling on the flat and over fences, and by hacking exercise. How the three elements are combined and in what proportion will depend upon the individual trainer and, also, upon the talent or otherwise of his pupil.

For the sake of clarity it is probably better to consider the work involved in each activity, although, of course, in practice the three would be blended into one programme.

The Lunge

In the work on the flat it should be possible to have the horse's side-reins at a shorter length for longer periods of time. The reins may also be attached higher up the roller, more nearly to the position of the hands than previously. It is usual to begin with the side-reins adjusted low down on each side of the roller to encourage the horse to lower the head, but in the final stages the head should be carried naturally in a position that allows for the reins to be fastened nearer to the withers. Otherwise the work on the flat will be aimed at perfecting the rhythm and elasticity of the paces and insisting upon the horse being correctly bent from poll to tail while executing a true circle.

Additionally, the lunge can be used to improve the canter, which as yet will be undeveloped. Initially, the horse will find cantering a true circle difficult to accomplish in a collected fashion and he may also have problems in striking-off correctly from trot into the canter pace. To strike-off correctly on the circle left the horse has to lead with his left, inside foreleg and vice versa when on the circle right. Leading with the outside foreleg is cantering 'false' and, until such time as the horse is sufficiently advanced the canter will be unbalanced and the horse in danger of falling over his own legs if not of causing some strain to them. Later, when the balance is much improved, the horse is expected to canter with the outside leg leading and remain in balance. The exercise is then termed the 'counter' canter. But for the moment the strike-off and the subsequent circle at canter is the objective. A relatively painless method of getting the correct strike-off, followed initially by a few strides of canter, is to place a single cavalletto across the corner of the school. The horse is then lunged over the small obstacle from trot and will almost always, because of the curve imposed, land in the canter stride and on the correct lead. Once the strike-off is established, progress can be made towards the cantering of a full circle to either hand.

Jumping ability is also improved by lungeing the horse over fences. This encourages the horse's confidence and initiative.

Fences should be firm and very solid but not, in the beginning, higher than 75cm (2.5ft) or so, and with a corresponding spread. Flimsy fences, easily knocked down, discourage good jumping. The horse soon loses respect for fences he knows will collapse at a slight knock and ceases, quite sensibly, to exert much effort in jumping them.

To help the horse judge the fence a 'distance' pole, or a low cavalletto, can be placed on the ground 9.9m (33ft) away. This distance, in fact, allows for two non-jumping canter strides between landing over the small fence and taking off over the larger one. An additional advantage in using a 'distance' pole is that it helps prevent the horse from acquiring the habit of rushing at his fences.

If the horse uses himself insufficiently over a fence and makes the angle of descent too steep, a pole placed a foot or so out on the landing side will encourage him to stretch out so as to clear the additional part of the obstacle. Conversely, a horse that gets too close at take-off to his fence can be helped by a pole or cavalletto placed on the take-off side.

When the horse is jumping a simple obstacle like this one freely and with confidence, new fences can be introduced which will cause, because of their construction or appearance, different problems. It is, in fact, no bad plan to make unusual looking fences. Coloured sacks laid over a fence or brightly coloured fertilizer cans surmounted by coloured poles make fences look sufficiently unusual and cause the horse to be given something to think about.

As jumping on the lunge progresses, combination fences can be used to increase the horse's judgement of the jump involved. The fences comprising a combination should, however, be placed at exactly the correct distances, otherwise the horse is being set too difficult a problem and will be in danger of becoming confused and of losing his confidence.

Between two vertical (upright) fences 7.2m (24ft) from inside to inside of each fence allows for one non-jumping stride at canter; 9.9m (33ft) allows for two strides. In the case of a vertical to a spread fence these distances have to be shortened by between 15cm (6in) and 30cm (12in) according to the length of the horse's stride and the speed at which the combination is approached. If the combination consists of a spread to a vertical then the distance between the two fences has to be lengthened by up to 30cm (12in).

In general terms a good stride at canter will cover 3.3m (11ft), and 3.6m (12ft) should be allowed for the leap from take-off to landing. Distances for three non-jumping strides are 13.5m (45ft); for four, 16.8m (56ft); and for five, 20.1m (67ft).

When using uprights to support fences there will obviously be a danger of the lunge becoming caught, with results that can be imagined. To avoid so disastrous a happening a pole is rested on the top of the upright from the ground on the take-off side and allowed to project some 45cm (18in) beyond the top of the upright. The rein will then slide up the pole without restraint.

As a general rule lungeing from the bit is not recommended and certainly it should not be countenanced when jumping from the lunge. On the other hand, there are methods of using the lunge rein from the bit which are acceptable enough in the hands of an expert and can be used beneficially. They can, indeed, replace the necessity for using long reins since by their use the horse can be 'put on the hand'.

Ridden Work on the Flat

The initial ridden school work in this stage is relatively undemanding of the horse and consists of establishing the pupil in the simpler school exercises, the changes of rein, shallow curves and occasional full circles using half of the school area. But in all these the direct rein of opposition is now used in preference to the elementary direct or opening rein. The effect of this rein, which acts on the quarters to alter the direction of the forward movement, ensures that the horse is bent round a turn along the whole length of his body, thus improving the lateral suppleness.

So far the horse has learned that the aids *act* to cause one movement or another, and *yield* when the movement is obtained. It is now necessary for him to be taught the third function of the aids, and to learn that they may also be used to *resist*. A simple example of a resisting aid is that of the outside leg on a turn. The leg held flat against the horse and to the rear of the girth prevents the quarters swinging too far out. It is then supporting the action of the inside leg and by holding the quarters may be said to be resisting their movement.

Similarly, the hands can resist, even if they must do so with infinite tact. In the beginning, the hands become more definite in their action only to prepare the horse for turns or transitions of pace, but in time they are used in conjunction with the legs to shorten the outline of the horse, helping to compress him towards his centre. By practising slow-ups (shortenings) and speed-ups (lengthenings), longitudinal suppleness of the horse is improved. The method employed is for the rider to continue the action of his legs while resisting intermittently with the fingers. The legs maintain the thrust forward of the quarters at one end, while the hands hold, or resist, that impulsion at the other.

Such exercises are performed for the most part at the trot; the sitting trot is employed only when a shortening of the horse is demanded. They have the effect of raising the head, lightening the forehand of the horse. This takes place because there is greater engagement of the hindlegs under the body and so the horse's weight is carried more upon the quarters and less upon the forehand. The raising of the head, involving the transference of body weight and balance a little to the rear and more over the quarters, is accomplished not by any upward action of the hands but by the increasing use of the legs, causing greater engagement of the horse's hind legs.

Those exercises that stretch the neck and lower the head are not, however, neglected. It is only by the stretching of the neck muscles that they are made able to contract, and they must contract when the head is carried in a higher position. (A singular property of muscle is that it can contract only to the degree that it can be stretched. It follows therefore that the horse's muscles must be stretched before they can be asked to contract effectively). Exercises over a grid of poles or cavalletti encourage this stretching and relaxation of the neck muscles, as well as helping to strengthen the quarters.

When the more complex school exercises can be accomplished, the head carriage will improve and the trainer will work towards the third element of L'Hotte's dictum – straightness. That quality will not be achieved in its entirety during this secondary stage but much progress can be made towards it. He will start by lightening both ends of the horse and the root of that is in the mobility of the quarters. The horse has to be taught first to move his quarters laterally, away from the action of a single leg, and finally to move his quarters round his forelegs in a *turn on the forehand*, another movement which will not be accomplished perfectly in the secondary stage of training.

This turn, like the *turn on the haunches*, is not a natural one. It is an example of man improving upon nature to further his own purposes. Horses in freedom turn on their centres. Very occasionally, if frightened, they may execute a turn on the quarters but never a turn on the forehand. These movements, however, mark the difference between the partially schooled horse and the much more responsive schooled one.

The reason why mobility of the quarters is taught is (1) to lighten the quarters, (2) to

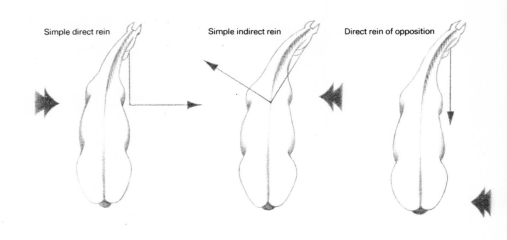

Simple direct rein   Simple indirect rein   Direct rein of opposition

The five rein effects. The closed arrows point to the main movement; the open ones to the secondary movement.

strengthen and make supple each hindleg individually by causing the hindlegs to cross, (3) to obtain control of the quarters, the origin of directional movement, and therefore of the horse himself. Most sources of resistance, perhaps surprisingly, emanate from the quarters rather than from elsewhere.

Methods used vary from trainer to trainer and from country to country but of them all the French method has the most logical appeal and is to be recommended because of its insistence on the maintenance of forward movement.

The first step is for the trainer, standing slightly to the side of the head and facing the tail, to hold the horse and then to walk backwards. He slows the horse a little, inclines the head a trifle towards him, then taps the horse low down behind the girth with his long whip. Inevitably the horse moves away from the whip and shifts the quarters over. He may, indeed, cross the hindlegs once or twice. The horse is then walked forward on the line dictated by the new position of the quarters. There is no point in teaching the horse to move in this fashion at halt since it is when the horse is in movement that it is necessary to be able to control the position of his quarters. Practised to either hand, after a few days this exercise should be easily executed from the saddle and it can then be followed by riding a zig-zag down the long side of the school before moving on to the *reversed half-volte*, the final lead-in to the actual forehand turn. The reversed half-volte is made by leaving the track on an oblique line and returning to it by a small 6m (24ft) half circle. In time the half-circle can be reduced in size until, eventually, a half-turn on the forehand can be executed.

When the head carriage is sufficiently high, the horse can be taught the *turn on the quarters*, which will lighten the forehand just as the preceding turn lightened the quarters. Until, however, the head is carried high enough the turn cannot be attempted. A low head carriage resists any lightening effect because it will not allow enough of the weight to be moved to the rear – an essential in the execution of the turn. The French term for this high carriage of the head is *ramener* and it refers to a head carried

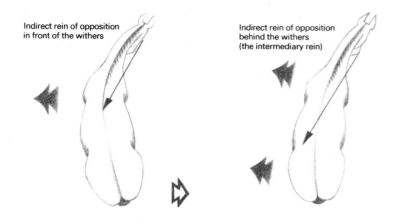

Indirect rein of opposition in front of the withers

Indirect rein of opposition behind the withers (the intermediary rein)

close to the vertical with the poll at the apex. It is a position brought about by *the advance of the body towards the head,* the former being driven forward on to gently resisting hands and it is the aim of progressive schooling. It will not be reached within the secondary education but at its completion the goal should be in sight.

The turn on the quarters follows the forehand turn because the former demands that the rider's legs must resist to hold them in place, whereas in the turn on the forehand the leg acted. It follows that an unwanted shift of the quarters cannot be opposed, and the quarters held in position for a turn to be made on them, until the horse has learned to move his quarters in obedience to the single leg as in the forehand turn. By teaching a horse to yield to a single leg the rider is provided with the means by which the horse will respond to one that resists.

The turn is taught in order to:
1) Eradicate the resistances of the quarters through being able to control them.
2) To make supple the shoulders as the forehand turn made supple the quarters.
3) To effect a re-balance of the horse. The forehand turn lightened the quarters, the turn on the quarters acts in opposite fashion to lighten the forehand. Both will therefore contribute to an overall improvement in balance.

Of the two the turn on the quarters is by far the most difficult and calls for the aids of hand and leg to be applied with exactitude and delicacy if the quarters are to be held in place and the forehand to pivot correctly round them. Nonetheless the approach to the turn, or at least to the half-turn on the quarters, can be made with a fair hope of success within the period of the secondary schooling.

As in the forehand turn the approach is made from walk but this time into a *half-volte*, the opposite to the reversed half-volte. Once more, the turn can, by degrees, be tightened until the point is reached where a half-turn on the quarters can be executed.

The lunge work will have prepared the horse for the cantering exercises under saddle and once the pace is established reasonably well on the lunge, the rider can begin cantering

in the school area. In the beginning the horse is bound to experience some little difficulty and this may also be the case in strike-offs into canter on the correct lead. The classical aids for the strike-off are the 'diagonal' aids i.e. for circle left the left rein and right leg (together, of course with the supporting right rein and the left leg at the girth). In many cases it is possible to obtain a strike-off perfectly well using these aids but if the horse has difficulty, the rider must resort to the 'lateral' aids, which are not pretty but do cause the horse to canter off correctly, even if he does so from a state of imbalance. The lateral aids for a canter lead to the left are the right hand drawing the head away from the direction of the movement and the strong application of the leg on the same side. The result of moving the head to the outside is to free the horse's inside shoulder, and it is then very difficult for him to do otherwise than lead with the inside leg. As the departures into canter become more proficient the gradual change to diagonal aids can be effected and will produce a more balanced transition.

Much work will need to be done to perfect the canter but it is most necessary that the pace is performed correctly, as the canter is probably *the* most useful pace for improving the longitudinal suppleness of the horse.

A simple form of control at the canter, producing either a shortening or lengthening of the posture, is easily practised by manipulating the reins. To extend the horse, for instance, the outside rein can be used to turn the nose slightly away from the directional movement. The effect will be to give greater freedom to the inside shoulder and to allow the stride made by the inside, leading, foreleg to be lengthened. To shorten the stride the inside rein must act and will by closing, or restricting, the full movement of the inside shoulder, shorten the stride. This simple technique is of great value in jumping a course of obstacles when it will always be necessary to control the length of stride in order to cope with the demands of the course and the individual fences.

Shortening the stride causes a re-imposition of balance and checks the impulsion by the weight being moved towards the quarters. It will, however, be necessary to teach the horse a more sophisticated method of achieving the same object by means of the *half-halt*, a movement which can also be used when making any downward transition or to check impulsion within the other paces. This is, however, most effective when practised at canter and, apart from being a very useful exercise in obedience, has a practical application in controlling the impulsion when jumping.

A half-halt means exactly that. It is a momentary check causing a redistribution of weight by shifting this from the forehand to the quarters. It will always be followed immediately by forward movement.

To make the half-halt the rider applies both legs in a strong momentary action, causing the horse to be sent further into contact with his bit. Almost simultaneously both hands are raised and turned upwards with the palms on top. The actions involve only a second or two and, obviously, it will be essential for the horse to be in strong impulsion before they can take effect. Without impulsion there would be nothing to check and no half-halt would be possible.

Further exercises in balance are involved in practising the transitions upwards and downwards from halt. These also provide a useful solution to an over-exuberant young horse.

In this stage attention will be paid to the correctness of the 'school' halt. The 'school' halt is accomplished when the horse stands square with fore and hindlegs together. Halted in this manner the horse is at once in a state of balance and is able to move off smoothly from that state. Occasionally a young horse will find it easy enough to bring his forelegs into line but will carry one hindleg behind its partner. The difficulty will be overcome by making the halt on an element of a circle, when the inside hindleg will be brought further under the body. If the problem is with the left hindleg a halt on a circle to the left will be used and vice versa.

Somewhat surprisingly, it may seem, no mention has yet been made of the *rein-back*, apart from the reference to the training in the stable when the horse was required to step back a pace or two from a push on his nose. The movement is delayed until this late stage for very good reasons. In the first place it is a difficult movement to perform correctly, and, secondly, it cannot be taught with any hope of success before the horse is in the correct form, has good engagement of the hocks and is confirmed in forward movement; nor can the horse rein-back from anything other than a square halt. Most trainers will teach the rein-back from the ground before attempting the movement from the saddle and risking the horse becoming confused. The horse is led down the side of the school, slowed down and brought to a square halt. The trainer then moves to the front and holding the reins in either hand causes the horse to lower his head. He will then act alternately with each rein towards the rear and the horse will usually take a pace back – if he does not, a tread on the horse's toes will produce the required result. The rein-back is in 'two-time', that is, the horse·moves his legs in diagonal pairs. It is *not* a walk backwards, since the walk is a pace of 'four-time'. The pace taken to the rear must, therefore, be made by a diagonal pair of legs moving in unison. Two paces are considered sufficient at this point and the horse must then be persuaded to move smartly forwards.

When the horse moves back in-hand in a straight line the exercise is carried out from the saddle, again using the wall to ensure that the quarters will not swing out in at least one direction. The horse will be ridden into halt, the legs will hold him straight and the hands will act alternately as before. Correctly done the horse should step back with the right fore and the left hind in response to the right rein and with the opposite diagonal when the left rein is applied.

Not all schools of thought will follow this method, or even agree with it, holding that if the horse is driven forward by the legs onto closed hands he must, since he cannot go forward, move backwards. It sounds logical enough but it is far, far more difficult to put into practice than the method described.

Finally the horse will learn something of the work on two tracks which will confirm the suppleness of his body. Two-track work, where the forelegs and hindlegs follow separate tracks begins with the exercise invented by the 18th Century French Master, de la Gironière. It is known as 'shoulder-in'. From this movement the horse will be taught the *half-pass*, in which he will move diagonally with his outside legs crossing over the inside ones. Two-track work has its roots in the training on the circle, with the horse correctly bent in the direction in which he is travelling, and in the turns on forehand and quarters which gave control over the quarters.

In shoulder-in the horse is bent from poll to tail with his head held *away* from the direction of the movement. He travels sideways but moves forward always in the direction of his convex side. The legs of the opposite concave side pass in front and cross over those of the convex side.

To perform the movement it is necessary to employ the more advanced rein aids, the indirect rein of opposition in front of the withers and the indirect rein of opposition behind the withers, sometimes known as the intermediary rein. The first of these acts to move the shoulders sideways, the second has the effect of moving the whole horse in a similar fashion. This latter is that most concerned with lateral work.

Shoulder-in is obtained from a circle, when the horse will be already correctly bent and prepared for the movement. In the case of left shoulder-in, a circle to the left is ridden and as the horse comes to the wall, the bend is held and the left intermediary rein applied behind the withers in the direction of the right hip, just as the forelegs are leaving the track and while the hindlegs are still on it. The right hand, after yielding initially, supports in line with the neck; the right leg, behind the girth, controls any swing of the quarters to the right while the left acts on the girth to maintain impulsion and reinforce the action of the left rein which, by opposing, is driving the quarters to the right. After a few steps have been executed the horse is pushed forward onto the circle again.

Clearly, the half-pass can be taught, and frequently is, from shoulder-in but it is probably best approached from the movement called *travers* which in English is called *head-to-the-wall* or, confusingly, *quarters-in*. It is probably easier to return to the half-volte which led up to the half-turn on the quarters, riding the figure with quarters-in and returning to the track by a few steps at half-pass. The advantage lies in the fact that forward movement will be promoted rather than slowed down, a tendency and a failing apparent in the conventional head-to-wall exercise preceding half-pass.

The aids for half-pass to the left in this case, applied as the return to the track is begun, are right rein on the neck (the indirect rein) and right leg held behind the girth, which will push the shoulders to the left. The left rein then inclines the head to the left while the left leg on the girth maintains the impulsion.

Once half-pass is obtained in this way it can be obtained on a straight line from the conventional head-to-the-wall movement, the horse being moved obliquely at first, no more than an angle of 25 to 30 degrees, and only later increasing the angle to 45 degrees. Head-to-the-wall is then followed by tail-to-the-wall *(renvers),* the opposite way round, so that the movement can be carried out independently of the wall.

Most schooling fences will have 'wings' or some form of side pole to prevent the horse from running out, but while 'wings' are helpful to start with, the aim should be to dispense with their aid by gradual stages.

To discourage the annoying habit of rushing and to encourage the horse to jump calmly, an exercise commencing with a single cavalletto is frequently carried out. The cavalletto is placed in the centre of the schooling area and approached from trot. The obstacle is jumped and then the horse is brought immediately to halt by the rider stretching his back upwards and inclining the shoulders a little to the rear on landing. The exercise, over two cavalletti, placed one on top of the other, can be extended to the canter pace and the horse halted on landing as before.

A variation on the same theme is to construct a square of cavalletti, the length and breadth being 9.9m (33ft). The square can be approached at trot, the obstacle jumped and the halt made in the centre. Then the horse can be

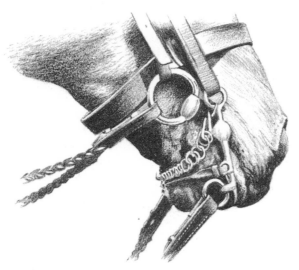

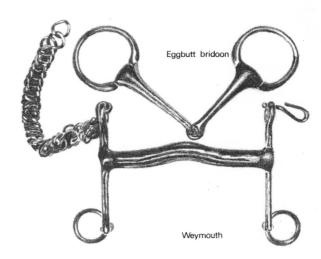
Eggbutt bridoon

Weymouth

The double bridle is a combination of the bridoon or snaffle bit and the curb or Weymouth bit.

Jumping

Once more the horse has been prepared for mounted jumping by the work on the lunge and to a large degree the ridden jumping follows the same pattern. Other exercises can, however, be practised and it is helpful if a jumping area is available where the horse can jump a variety of obstacles and where once a week or so in the later stages of training he can be asked to jump one, or at the most two, bigger fences. On one thing all trainers are agreed, and that is that (1) good jumping is the result of sound, basic training on the flat, (2) that, within reason, the less jumping that a horse does the better he will jump – it is all too easy and too tempting to overjump a horse and make him sour.

Cross-country type fences, particularly those involving jumping from one level to another and, of course, water should be included in the jumping training. A good way to teach a horse to jump the latter is to lay a pole or cavalletto on the take-off side and place a pole over the centre of the spread. This will make the horse gain some height in his leap and helps him to realize that water does, in fact, constitute a fence to be jumped.

jumped out over the cavalletto immediately in front of him or, later on, he can be asked to make a right or left turn and jump out of the sides of the box.

As a practical accomplishment and one that also encourages confidence, obedience and initiative, the horse should also be taught to jump from an angle, something he will certainly be required to do if he is ever to jump seriously in competition.

As before, a cavalletto is laid in the centre of the school and jumped from a straight approach at trot. Very gradually the approach is made at an increasing angle until the horse is being ridden in a figure of eight with the cavalletto at its centre. Another cavalletto placed alongside the first to make a spread can then be jumped from canter in the same manner, the leading leg being changed at each end of the school by bringing the horse back to trot for a few paces before striking off on the appropriate leg. An extension of these exercises is possible by making use of the cavalletti square which can be jumped in a variety of ways.

The final exercise involves changing direction whilst jumping the fence and is obviously more difficult to accomplish. It is, however, an invaluable technique in jumping competitions. A small fence is erected and jumped first from a straight approach and then from a slight angle. In this last instance the horse will almost always land with the correct foreleg leading since he is to all intents on an element of a circle. If the fence is jumped slightly from the left the horse is on a right-handed circle and will land with the right foreleg leading. The bend can be increased by inclining the horse's head in the requisite direction while he is still in the air. In time, and with some practice, it will be possible to jump the fence from a straight approach and bend the horse to either direction over the obstacle according to the position of the next fence on the course.

In jumping competitions there is seldom time or opportunity for the rider to be concerned with the niceties of changing the lead, a great deal must, perforce, be left to the horse. Trained in this way, the horse will learn to change leg automatically when the direction is changed by the rider.

Hacking

Hacking during the secondary stage of training is of just as much importance as in the primary schooling. As well as relaxing the horse and keeping him interested it provides opportunities for teaching valuable lessons which cannot be taught in the school area. In the early periods the horse will learn to canter, often over undulating ground, and towards the end of the training he will be given short gallops, not only to improve his wind but to teach him to carry his rider at this much faster pace. Road work at a steady trot improves his muscular condition, helps his wind and hardens his legs and, of course, it is on the roads that he will learn about traffic. It is a wise precaution for the young horse to be accompanied by a 'school-master' but as time goes on less reliance will be placed upon the older horse and by the end of the training period the youngster should be fairly reliable in most types of traffic conditions.

The Double Bridle

Towards the end of the secondary training it will be necessary to introduce the horse to the double bridle. So far the horse will have been ridden in a plain jointed snaffle, with or without a drop noseband, but now he has to be taught to respond to the more sophisticated actions of the double bridle, which will help the flexion of the lower jaw and poll in a way that is not completely possible in a snaffle. The double bridle, indeed, will add to the polish of the educated horse. Nonetheless it is necessary for the horse to be taught to carry the bridle and to understand its actions.

The double bridle consists of a light bradoon lying in the mouth above a short-cheeked curb bit. The former in the trained horse acts upwards upon the corners of the lips to suggest a raising of the head. The curb, when it assumes, through the pressure of the rein, an angle of some 45 degrees, acts upon three parts of the head to induce a lowering and a retraction of the nose from the poll.

The mouthpiece of the bit has a port in its centre to allow room for the tongue and to ensure that the bearing surface rests on the bars of the mouth. The action is a downward one and slightly to the rear and is assisted by the curb chain acting on the curb groove. The combined effect of the two is to cause the horse to lower his head and flex the lower jaw while retracting his nose. This lowering influence of the bit is supported by pressure being applied to the *poll*. The latter occurs when rein pressure is applied causing the eye of the bit, which is attached to the cheekpieces, to move forward, thus exerting pressure through the cheekpieces to the headpiece of the bridle.

The two bits of the double bridle, therefore, enable the rider to position the head by raising it, lowering it and bringing the nose inwards. Unless the horse is accustomed to these complexities gradually he is more likely to resist the unfamiliar pressures than to respond to them.

The first lesson, as is often the case, takes place in the stable where the horse is fitted very carefully with the new bridle. He is then given a small feed still wearing the bridle. In order to eat he must relax his lower jaw and this is the first lesson. After some three or four days of wearing his bridle while eating a small feed, the bit can be manipulated in the mouth. To prevent the horse retreating from the pressures he is placed with his quarters into a corner. The reins are passed over the head and the trainer takes the bradoon rein in the left hand, holding it some 25cm (10 inches) from the bit rings and above the nose. The bit reins are held in the right hand, the same distance from the bit, but behind the horse's chin. The head is raised a few times by the bradoon and the curb rein is operated to make the horse drop his nose and relax his lower jaw.

When the horse understands what is wanted and is responding to the action of both reins, the lesson can be carried out in the school with the trainer holding the reins as before and walking backwards while an assistant follows the horse to keep him moving forward.

Finally, the reins are put over the neck and the trainer positions himself at the near-side with the bradoon rein in his right hand and the curb in his left. The same raising and lowering exercises are practiced at the halt and, by manipulating the reins, the trainer will ask the horse to flex to the right and left. When this can be done at halt it is carried out at walk and after a week or so it should be possible to ride the horse satisfactorily in the bridle.

The methods which have been described are not common to all trainers, each will have his own ways developed from his personal experience. But if the detail differs, most trainers would agree on the general progression followed and that such training, properly carried out will produce what every rider wants, a sound, strong, reliable all-round horse.

Show Jumping and Eventing

PAMELA MACGREGOR-MORRIS

Students of equestrianism, especially within the last twenty years during which time a well defined line of demarcation has come into existence between the different branches of riding, often decide to specialize once they have reached a certain general level of achievement.

A great deal, of course, depends upon how seriously they take their riding. The less competitive minded, and those who are fortunate enough to live in or near a good hunting country, will generally settle for hunting, incomparably still the best of all horse sports, with perhaps a few rides in point-to-points and hunter trials added for good measure.

The more ambitious, if they have the time and the money to spare, will branch out into combined training or show jumping. The former sport is apt to attract the countryman, while the suburban rider more often gets drawn towards show jumping. Owing to the active participation of H.R.H. Princess Anne and Captain Mark Phillips, and the attendant and inevitable publicity which the media have showered upon them, even the most confirmed pedestrians are now able to distinguish between the sport which is honoured by royal patronage and that in which the most publicized and controversial rider is Harvey Smith.

Show jumping, certainly in the top echelons, is very much a specialist sport in which only a handful of riders can contrive or afford to remain amateur. The schooling and the practice are time-consuming, and without a constant amount of both, no one can hope to succeed. The true show jumping horse, moreover, is something of a freak of nature. He will not get very far in the sport today unless he is capable of negotiating six foot in height without difficulty. He is thus comparatively rare, and as such commands a top price, in common with every other commodity which is greatly sought after and in short supply. Phil Oliver, whose son Alan has been one of the leading riders since the end of the second World War, once told me that it was by no means unusual to buy two thousand horses and not find a show jumper among them; for not only must the jump be there, it must also be accompanied by a calm, generous and courageous

temperament, sound limbs, and a hardy constitution.

The technique of riding a show jumper is highly skilled and specialized. It demands a standard of riding, training and production which is beyond the capacity of the average rider. Practically all the top riders, particularly in England, have come up through the junior and young riders classes, and have got their eye in at an early age. Riding a show jumper is only for the dedicated, with plenty of time at their disposal, for only practice makes perfect.

Although the same can be said, by and large, of the top combinations in combined training, which involves three distinct and different disciplines – dressage, cross-country and show jumping – it is much more a sport for the amateur. It is designed to comprise the complete test of horse and rider and is thus aimed at the all-round horse, stopping short of Grand Prix dressage, Grand National or Nations' Cup standards. It is thus within the compass of most well-bred horses with temperaments calm enough to do the dressage, sufficiently bold to go across country, and sufficiently supple and sound to jump a small and twisting course of show jumping fences on the third day, after a gruelling 20-mile speed and endurance test. This endurance test involves two sections of roads and tracks (no jumping), a steeplechase course and upwards of 30 big, solid cross-

PREVIOUS PAGE A colourful scene in the collection ring of a show jumping competition. David Broome and Harvey Smith compare notes before an event.

BELOW Activity after a round.

country fences, many of them with problems of approach or with alternative methods of negotiation, of which the fastest will be the most difficult.

Even at Olympic level, the world's top eventing teams are all indisputably amateur in composition. The British, who won the gold medals in Mexico in 1968 and retained them at Munich in 1972, comprised a retired cavalry Major, a Staff-Sergeant in Remounts, a student nurse, the daughter of a Brigadier, a serving cavalry officer and a business consultant. The latter, Richard Meade, holder of the individual gold medal, goes for morning runs around Hyde Park, in central London, in order to keep fit, before embarking upon a strenuous day at his office.

Strangely enough, several of the world's top show jumping riders started their careers in the Three-Day Event before progressing to the more rarefied atmosphere of international show jumping, which they found to be more demanding. The distinguished Raimondo d'Inzeo first represented Italy in a Three-Day Event, while Fritz Ligges, team gold medallist in the Olympic Prix des Nations in Munich, 1972, won the Olympic individual bronze medal, riding Donkossak in Tokyo in 1964. D'Inzeo's Olympic debut was in 1948 at Aldershot where, riding a horse called Regate, he was 30th individually (from a field of 46) for the Three-Day Event. At Helsinki four years later, his elder brother Piero was sixth individually on Pagoro, and riding for the Canadian team was another future show jumping gold medallist, Tom Gayford, who captained the winning Prix des Nations team in Mexico in 1968.

Now the two different disciplines are far more segregated, in every nation. David Broome once told me that he would not ride round Badminton, chiefly because of the dressage test, but he also marvelled at the people who rode over the cross-country fences. 'They must be all guts or no brains!' he added. In the Munich Olympics, when the British team were leading the field in the Three-Day Event, with only the show jumping still to go, the British show jumping team were not at all sanguine about their chances. 'They are not much good at show jumping,' they said of their mounts.

The Eventers went on to win, regardless, but it must be admitted that one often realizes just how good at their own particular sport the show jumpers are when one watches the event riders, so bold and brilliant over solid cross-country fences, tackling a small, straightforward course of artificial fences.

Where to Start

With the growth and the success of the junior championships which are now held in most parts of the world, competitions for young and novice riders and horses are so prevalent, preceded in many countries by Pony Club competitions, that large numbers of young people are able to acquire a solid grounding in

A cross-country competitor in Switzerland. The horse is wearing rubber overreach boots as well as exercise bandages for protection.

riding and horsemanship which can take them to advanced levels without any particular financial privileges. Those who do not come from a background of horses, and who do not have their own horse, will have to work harder in order to ride, but some of our best riders have started their careers without any pecuniary advantages, working in stables as grooms during the early stages. Any young man or woman can, given the ability and sufficient determination, make a success of an equestrian career, though it will take a little longer to arrive.

There are, in any case, no short cuts to success. Given the essential flair – which basically means a sympathy with horses – the rest all hinges upon a receptive mind, a willingness to learn and a capacity for hard work.

For those fortunate enough to own their horse – which ideally for competition work should be either a high-class hunter of 16–16·2hh. or a temperate Thoroughbred – the groundwork is the same, whether the goal be jumping or eventing. There is no substitute for sound schooling on the flat to achieve a supple and obedient horse, whatever his job in life.

This achieved, many combined training enthusiasts are firm believers in hunting their young horses for a season before putting them into competitive work. A horse that has

RIGHT A competitor from France in the jump known as the 'Coffin' at the Burghley Horse Trials. Several jumps on a cross-country course have two or three parts to them, often giving the competitor a choice of course through the obstacles. These may consist of a couple of different fences or low walls and a ditch set on a steep slope or at an angle.

RIGHT Lorna Sutherland on Peer Gynt in the Trout Hatchery at Burghley. The horses approach the stream down a hill, jump over a fence into water the other side, cross the stream and jump a log fence out. Obstacles are very solidly constructed and vary considerably; they may include tractor tyres, hay racks, bales and water troughs and are often positioned in thickets or on slopes. It takes a confident, highly trained horse to complete a course accurately and at speed.

followed hounds over a natural country learns to look after himself while enjoying himself vastly in the process. He will then be a far better, bolder and more reliable performer over a novice one-day event course than if all his experience had been gained in cold blood over artificial fences.

Mary Gordon-Watson hunted her World Champion and double Olympic team gold medallist, Cornishman V, in High Leicestershire; Martin Whiteley hunted – and still hunts – The Poacher, who helped to win an Olympic gold medal and a world and three European team titles; Richard Meade hunted Barberry and Jane Bullen hunted Our Nobby. In fact, the hunting field is responsible not only for Britain and Ireland's breeding the best event horses, but has played an invaluable part in their training, enabling them to take on and defeat the best horses from other lands. Bruce Davidson, who won the World Championship for the United States at Burghley in 1974, riding Irish Cap, is also a dedicated foxhunter, married to the daughter of a Master of Hounds in Pennsylvania.

Though Ann Moore hunted Psalm, her Olympic silver medallist, with the North Warwickshire in his youth, few of the show jumping fraternity have either the time or the inclination to hunt their horses. David Broome is an exception, being Joint-Master, with his father, of the Curre Hounds in Monmouthshire, and his lovely natural seat and beautiful hands, which have helped him to win two Olympic bronze medals, a world championship and three European titles, are far more typical of the hunting field than of the archetypal show jumper.

One successful Three-Day Event team which owes no debt to foxhunting, however, is that of Australia, which won the Olympic gold medals in Rome in 1960. Bill Roycroft, who captained the team for a decade, and was the first person to ride three horses around Badminton on the same day, was invited to hunt in Ireland a few years ago. I was astonished to learn that he did not consider hunting to be a great sport. When I pressed him to give a reason, he replied, without hesitation: 'Those damn silly dawgs!'

The early life of the budding show jumper is far more confined, comprising in the main an endless series of novice, Foxhunter and Freshmen's competitions, outdoors during the season proper and indoors during the winter, at one or other of the large covered schools which have proliferated since jumping became an all-the-year-round sport some years ago.

Show jumping is a sport in which extreme precision is all important, and though the moderate rider can take a good horse to a certain stage with happy results, by the time the horse has won sufficient prize money to be upgraded in the official records from C to B, the courses are bigger and the whole exercise becomes more difficult. When Grade A has been attained the courses are more demanding still, often with related fences and distance problems, and this is where the experts take over. To ride a horse over a single fence is within the scope of all. It is possible to keep out of trouble, at a low height, even when he has stood off too far, or 'put in a short one' or come in too close. Over big combination fences, a good eye for distance, a sense of timing and judgement of pace become all important, and the dilettante rider is no longer able to cope.

Fred Broome, David's father, likes to buy young horses that have been brought on slowly and carefully over small courses, as long as their owners know when they have reached their limit. 'Then is the time for them to sell, if they don't want to spoil a promising horse. They can sell the horse well enough to buy three or four more young ones, and start all over again with them.'

Few of the experts who are on the international circuit have time to bring on a young horse from scratch. But they can take over a half-made jumper and bring him to his peak. David Broome is particularly fortunate, not only in having his father's help and support, but also in having a younger brother and sister, Mary and Frederick, who can campaign the 'green' horses around the country shows in South Wales. For him, with all his experience of riding some of the best horses in the world, a green youngster is no fun at all. And many riders feel that it is impossible to combine, with any hope of success with either, the riding of horses who know their job with

A competitor takes the log pile at the Burghley World Championships.

BELOW Captain Mark Phillips in the Trout Hatchery at Burghley in 1974 when Burghley was the scene of the world Three-Day Event Championships which were won by the American team headed by Bruce Davidson on Irish Cap, with Michael Plumb on Good Mixture, E Emerson on Victor Dakin and Don Sachey on Plain Sailing. Mark Phillips and Columbus were leading the field for the individual title at the end of the cross-country day but had to withdraw because of an injury before the final showjumping phase.

the riding of those who do not. A completely different style and technique are required; even the attitude of mind is different.

Harvey Smith has his former school friend, Willie Halliday, to ride and school his young horses, and Fred Hartill keeps Paddy McMahon on Pennwood Forgemill. The youngsters are produced by others of his team. The Americans bring young horses to tour the European shows three years in every four, but they are confined to the young riders and have been well schooled during the previous winter at their training centre at Gladstone, New Jersey, by their brilliant coach, Bertalan de Nemethy.

I think that the most basic difference between show jumping and three-day eventing is

that, whereas the former is entirely artificial, the latter – give or take a few of the Normandy Bank type of cross-country fences – is more or less natural. No horse left to itself would ever, of its own volition, twist and turn to jump some 17 closely-related fences in a small arena in under two minutes; but they can and they do jump fences between fields, boundary fences and walls on parkland, and even water ditches where these form the natural boundaries.

RIGHT Bill Steinkraus competing in the 1971 Nations Cup at Hickstead.

BELOW RIGHT Captain Raimondo d'Inzeo and Talky in the Wills Embassy Regal Stakes at Hickstead 1974.

RIGHT Alison Dawes schooling a young horse at home over a jump on the lunge. This teaches the horse to jump freely before having to cope with the weight and balance of the rider.

BELOW H.R.H. Princess Anne riding Goodwill in the dressage test at the European Three-Day Event Championships at Luhmuhlen, Germany in September 1975. They were placed second.

Countries and their Achievements

Colonel Hans-Heinrich ('Mickey') Brinckmann, former German cavalry officer and international rider, then team trainer, now one of the world's leading coursebuilders, is convinced that show jumping courses should be kept as natural as possible. Though he is best known as the fence architect at Aachen, he is not wholly in favour of the arena-type show, preferring the Hickstead-type course with banks, stone walls, table jumps and Devil's Dykes – though he emphasizes that they are too tiring to the horse to be jumped as a regular diet.

The Germans are, of course, the top show jumping nation in the world. Britain generally succeeds in monopolizing the President's Cup, the World Team Championship, although the United States and West Germany have won it twice and three times respectively since Prince Philip, Duke of Edinburgh, president of the I.E.F., first presented it in 1965. But the Germans have won the Olympic Prix des Nations, which still rates above all else in prestige, on no fewer than four occasions since the second World War, four times, in fact, in seven Olympic Games, and they did not compete in the first postwar Olympics.

There are two main reasons for the dominance of the German team. Their horses are immensely powerful and have a comparatively phlegmatic temperament that makes them accept a rigorous system of training which would be resented by high couraged animals with more thoroughbred blood in them. Instant obedience and utter submissiveness are the keynotes, and though both qualities are desirable to a point, beyond that point the horse is robbed of his initiative, with the result that when things go wrong he is unable to assist. British, American and Italian riders, who comprise the other great show jumping nations, endeavour to produce a harmonious partnership between mount and man, an interdependent relationship which entails generous co-operation rather than slavish obedience.

However, for show jumping the German system certainly produces results, for, oddly enough, the German horses are not possessed of an enormous natural jump but of a jump which can be produced to a pitch of near-infallibility. The horses who won the gold medals in Munich were uniformly consistent. They won not because one or two jumped brilliant clear rounds, but because they all got round with a maximum of eight faults, or two fences down in each round.

The Italians, whose Federico Caprilli revolutionized the art and science of jumping fences by propounding the forward seat in the early years of this century, rely chiefly for their successes upon the legendary d'Inzeo brothers, Piero and Raimondo, respectively a Colonel in the Tank Corps and a Major in the Carabinieri, the Mounted Police. The two sons of a rough-riding sergeant in the cavalry rely

BELOW All competitors' horses are given a veterinary examination in between every stage of a Three-Day Event and only horses passed as sound and fit continue. A check is particularly important after the second day – the cross-country.

BELOW RIGHT Richard Meade on The Poacher – one of the most successful eventers of the last few years. Richard Meade won the Gold Medal in the Munich Olympic Games on Laurieston.

upon Irish-bred horses, on whom their greatest victories have been achieved. Where some of the Germans school their horses in draw reins, strapped up (or rather, down) like suitcases, they use their hands to achieve balance and collection, and their flowing style is in the classical idiom.

The Americans, thanks to Bert de Nemethy, are even more classical and could be held up to all the young as a pattern to be emulated as regards seat, hands and position. They are stylish to a man and effective. They won the team silver medals in the last Olympics, as they did in Rome in 1960. In Mexico City in 1968, their captain, Bill Steinkraus, took the individual gold on Snowbound.

Who Show Jumps?

Professionalism in the top international circles has long been a vexed subject, and it was brought to a head in 1972 when, at the General Assembly of the F.E.I. in Brussels, Prince Philip called upon show jumping to put its house in order. Britain gave a lead and now has 43 professionals under licence, among them David Broome and Harvey Smith, each of them a sad loss to Britain's Olympic effort. But, sad to relate, no other nation has seen fit to follow this shining example, and it seems highly unlikely that one ever will. Just how the affair will resolve itself by the time the next Olympic Games take place seems very much a matter of conjecture.

On the continent of Europe, show jumping has always been a far more prestigious sport than it is in England. With no foxhunting to occupy the long winter, those who wished to ride resorted to dressage and show jumping competitions – not just the cavalry officers, but the nobility as well. But in England, where there was not only hunting but steeplechasing and polo, there was already a more than sufficient choice of things to do with a horse. Thus, though cavalry officers from Weedon, Woolwich and Netheravon show jumped as part of their curriculum, the sport has never attracted many civilians, save those who could be termed professionals, with a few sporting farmers, small dealers and business people.

With the phasing-out of the cavalry officer, who has exchanged his horse for a tank, the show jumping elite are now entirely drawn from a new walk of life. Apart from the hard core who stem from agriculture – the sons of hunting farmers such as the Broomes, Ted Edgar, Graham Fletcher and Rowland Fernyhough – many are from families who have made money since the war, and are often new to horses. But they tend to come and go; originally attracted to the sport by what they believe to be the glamour, eventually disenchanted by the discovery that the glamour is ephemeral but the hard slog, the pitfalls and the disappointments, are always there. Only the hard core, the very backbone of the sport, are still there year after year, taking the rough with the smooth, looking beyond the lean times when they are short of a good horse to the

future when their luck will surely change.

Often – all too often – the newcomers who blow like a whirlwind across the sport, to be hailed by the media as brilliant, turn out to be one-horse riders. When that one horse has shot its bolt they tend to disappear from the scene, leaving others to take their place. One has to be really dedicated to soldier on in adversity, in the knowledge that each rider will be privileged to find just one really great horse in his career; and that he will spend the rest of his life looking for another.

So what persuades a girl or a young man to go 'on the circuit', travelling the country from early spring to late autumn in a horse box, living in the caravan it tows? Idyllic, perhaps, in good weather for the young; but what of the shows where the rain never stops and gales blow, where the ground is a quagmire and horses and humans are caked in mud? To enjoy, or even to tolerate this sort of life week after week and year after year, demands a special sort of dedication, in which stoicism also plays a leading part.

The horse trials scene is a great deal less spartan. A horse will compete in only a couple of Three-Day Events, which by their duration mean a few days spent away from home each year. The one-day event, where his preparation is accomplished, comprises a horse trial which is completed between morning and early evening. In the Spring or Autumn season it is quite possible to find an event within reasonable

distance on Saturdays, so that the rider can hold down a job in addition to training his horse. During the summer weekends, the horse can improve his show jumping by competing in the novice competitions at small shows, or in dressage tests at Riding Club fixtures. The whole approach is completely amateur and not in the least pressurized, the horse, as an all-rounder rather than a specialist, will be cheaper to buy, and the emphasis is upon training in every department.

Bruce Davidson of the United States, the new World Champion, is a 24-year-old New Englander who started riding seriously at his preparatory school. He was selected to train with the team by Bert de Nemethy in nation-

wide screening trials and has sufficient means to live without taking a job, though he is building up a farm with brood mares and young horses. While most young men ride in events for the thrill of the speed and endurance phase, he even enjoys the dressage – the result, he maintains, of its being made so interesting by the French-bred team trainer, Jack Le Goff, who is himself the product of the French Cavalry School at Saumur. He is also very interested in show jumping, and show jumped his horse, Irish Cap, in 1975, before starting his preparation for the next Olympic Games.

Purchase and Training of Competition Horses

The cheapest and most satisfactory horses for the aspiring competition rider to buy are green four-year-olds that have been well broken and ridden. If they have been hunted, so much the better. But green horses can easily be spoiled by novice riders, who, unless they can bring them on with the constant supervision of an expert, would be better advised to pay rather more for something that knows its job, or has at least been well versed in its rudiments.

Although, for the young particularly, there is nothing to touch the Thoroughbred horse except the really high-class hunter, who may well be seven-eighths clean bred, discarded race horses are seldom suitable for any but the most experienced riders. Only seldom have

they been carefully and methodically mouthed, broken and schooled, and they often require to be re-made; while the whole process of discovering that they are not good enough to train on is often fairly traumatic. They will have been hotted-up on the gallops at just that period in their development when it pays to hasten slowly, and if they have got as far as the race course they will already have acquired a built-in reluctance to being overtaken, which will make them pain and grief to hunt and often even to ride in company.

Nor, as already mentioned in relation to buying a family horse, are sales a happy hunting ground for the uninitiated. So keep away from the auctioneer's hammer unless accompanied by your vet., lawyer, blacksmith, and father-confessor; the latter for the use of the vendor.

The reliable dealer who knows what you want is often the best source of supply, even though you may pay a little bit over the odds in the first instance. He will, if he values his reputation, stand behind his horse. If it turns out to be disappointing he will take it back and replace it with another. If you have sunk your all in the purchase of a useless quadruped that you cannot even ride it is comforting to know that all is not lost.

Horses bought off the farm tend to be far more reasonably priced than those bought out of novice jumping competitions or one-day events. There is no middle-man to take his cut,

BELOW Alwin Schockemohle of Germany is taking this fence very low. The horse is wearing studs in the back shoes to give him extra grip. They are screwed in and are essential if the course is greasy.

the horse has not been seen in public except possibly in the hunting field, and there is unlikely to be any question of being talked into buying the horse. It has been said, moreover, that there are fools, damn fools and those who breed horses. The breeder, who has taken all the chances, seldom if ever gets a worthy return for the fruits of his labours. He deserves to be able to sell direct to the consumer, rather than to the man who may only keep the horse for 24 hours before passing him on with at least 25% added to the original price.

The question of good and bad conformation is far too complex to be entered into within the scope of this article. The essentials are, first and foremost, good limbs and feet and straight action, a well sloped shoulder to give length of rein, a wide chest and depth of girth to give good heart room and stamina, and a long, low, springing stride. Good hind legs, which are the propelling force, and strong forelegs, with convex knees, to take the jar of landing over big or drop fences, are absolutely vital. No horse should ever be bought, except by the most expert, without a thorough examination by an independent or one's own veterinary surgeon. To have the horse on trial for a week is, in modern conditions, ideal but Utopian. In the unlikely event of such a concession being available, it is imperative to insure the horse for this period.

Getting the horse fit is a matter of slow work for increasing periods up to two hours daily, with faster work after the first eight weeks, and good feeding, with the corn ration increasing to the amount and type of work. Appearance and performance are the surest guides to condition. If the horse both looks well and goes well there is unlikely to be much amiss with the stable management.

The sort and degree of fitness that is required by the Three-Day Event horse is far in excess of that of the show jumper, whose job is done in one or two rounds which average two minutes in duration, although those two minutes involve some fifteen to seventeen great efforts in negotiating big fences. But the event horse has to go some 17 to 20 miles in the speed and endurance test, jumping on average forty fences. If he is not really fit he will blow up, or fall, or both on the cross-country. Lack of fitness is the cause of some 75% of the accidents which occur in Three-Day Events.

BELOW Frank Chapot of the USA on Mainspring in the final of the World Championship at Hickstead in 1974. Mainspring is wearing a breastplate and a running martingale and is well balanced over this formidable looking wall. Bricks are easy to dislodge despite their solid appearance.

Racing for All

HUGH CONDRY

Horse racing has probably been going on in some form or another since not long after man first discovered that the four-legged creatures who ran like the wind would accept him astride their backs. That was around 2000 BC, though horses had been domesticated and used as draught animals for about 3000 years before that. Whether riding developed gradually or was the consequence of some simple herdsman's sudden explosion of inspiration we can never know, but it was as important a step forward for mankind as was the discovery of powered flight 4000 years later. And once the art had been acquired, man's competitive instincts must have resulted, sometime, somewhere, in a 'beat-you-to-that-tall-tree' type challenge from one young horseman to another. But those far-off ancestors of ours were primarily concerned with the problems of survival. The ridden horse could help them in that, could help them hunt, help them escape danger, help them in battle, but as for racing . . . well, that would scarcely have rated very high in their natural scheme of things. How very different today.

Racing is carried on all over Europe but probably only two countries France and Italy can be considered as forces to be reckoned with in the international field, with Germany occupying the leading place amongst the racing nations of the second rank.

French racing follows the British pattern but most major meetings are held at weekends, with the big races being run almost entirely on Sundays. The French equivalent of the English classics are the Poules d'Essai and the Prix Royal Oak (the equivalents of the Guineas and the St. Leger, respectively) and the Prix du Jockey Club (the Derby). There is also an additional classic race run at Longchamp, the Grand Prix de Paris. Prize money in France is high and betting, to the benefit of the industry, is confined to the *pari-mutuel*, which operates on the fifty or so flat-racing tracks spread about the country, the best of which are modelled on the Longchamps course which was completely rebuilt in 1966. Prime instigator of the Longchamp development was the French millionaire industrialist and sportsman Marcel Boussac, and it is due largely to his financial and organising genius that French racing and breeding enjoys its present pre-eminence

Italy, whose Jockey Club was founded in 1880, has some thirteen race tracks and about 400 racing days during the season. The Thoroughbred population is small in comparison with the major racing countries, so much so that the contribution made by Italian horses must be regarded as being very much out of proportion to the size of the industry. Just as French racing owes so much to Marcel Boussac, so its Italian counterpart is indebted to Frederico Tesio, a breeder of incomparable skill who produced such horses as Navarro, who was a potent factor in the Dormello Stud pedigrees; Apelle, and probably two of the finest types of Thoroughbred ever produced in Donatello II and Nearco. Later, of course, there was the great Ribot. Essentially, the Italian Thoroughbred is a middle distance horse and it is such horses that have gained Italy a place in the forefront of the racing nations.

RIGHT In the paddock . . . the horses loosen up, the jockeys get nervous and the public bet.

West Germany, with much the same number of Thoroughbreds as Italy, is in comparison only a second rate power in the racing world and there seems little hope that the position will change. Only a limited number of German horses have made any sort of impact outside their own country in the past quarter of a century, the best being Bella Paola who won the 1,000 Guineas and Oaks and Champion Stakes in England in 1958. On the other hand, the best German races fall frequently to foreign horses.

Many countries in Europe run races over fences. France has steeplechasing at Auteuil, Fontainebleu, Pau and at one or two other sites, but nowhere has 'chasing risen above the level of a minor sport except in Britain and Ireland. There is, of course, the famous Gran Pardubice Steeplechase run in Czechoslovakia each October, but otherwise there is little of great note and in this sport Britain and Ireland are the acknowledged leaders and likely to remain so.

Racing in Britain

Today horse racing is the biggest single competitive equestrian activity of them all, employing – directly or indirectly, – the most people, turning over, and tying up, the greatest amount of money, using the most advanced veterinary technology and scientific breeding methods, and receiving the greatest news coverage and publicity. It rates, in fact, second only to football as Britain's national sport, and

contributes some £110 million annually to the exchequer via a tax on gambling, which, since the advent of licensed betting shops in 1961, has reached an almost obsessive level.

Money from the tax on horse race betting – paid by the gamblers, – goes straight into the Chancellor's national purse. The Betting Levy – a direct imposition on bookmakers but also taken indirectly from punters – is raised and distributed solely for the benefit of the racing industry, which received about seven million pounds from this source during 1974. This adverse ratio of about ten to one between the amount taken out of racing by the government and the amount put back in is considerably worse than in many other countries – in some it can be a straight one-for-one level – and is the principal reason why the sport, in the inflationary seventies, finds itself facing a major financial crisis.

Basically horse racing comes in two varieties, flat and National Hunt, though the latter – the jumping game, over the sticks, call it what you will – is subject to a further sub-division, as we shall see later on. Flat racing is by far the oldest. It was known in Ancient Egypt; there were contests for 'saddle horses' as well as chariots in the Olympic Games of the sixth and seventh centuries BC; and the sport was popular with the Romans, who introduced it to Britain. Nurtured here by noblemen in medieval times, the 'Sport of Kings' received a notable boost when it enjoyed the royal patronage of such as King Charles II and Queen Anne. It

was during Anne's reign that a new course was laid out as Ascot in Berkshire, now the scene, every June, of the most famous race meeting in the world, Royal Ascot. Moreover, to a considerable extent the otherwise insignificant town of Newmarket in Suffolk owes its position as the acknowledged headquarters of British racing to the keenness with which Charles II was wont to pursue his passion – for horses – on its magnificent galloping heathlands.

At Newmarket over 200 years ago the Jockey Club was born, first exercising its aristocratic and autocratic control over the conduct of racing there and, with the passing years, extending its influence to cover the length and breadth of the nation. British racing, its rules and its conduct, became the model for that established in many other countries, and the influence of British bloodstock was and still is felt the world over.

Before King Charles' day racehorses were not far removed from the animals which carried their owners about their everyday business, but since then horses have increasingly been bred specifically for racing. The greatest change occurred with the introduction of Eastern blood. Groups of mares were imported from Turkey and other lands bordering the eastern end of the Mediterranean, as well as several stallions, of whom the most famous are the Byerley Turk, the Darley Arabian and the Godolphin Arabian, all of whom reached these shores around the turn of the 17th century. Curiously these easterners do not appear to have achieved prominence in *racing*, yet their importation and crossing with indigenous stock resulted in nothing less than the establishment of a new breed, the Thoroughbred, which is now the basis of a major industry involving hundreds of studs whose total annual production of more than 8,000 foals is aimed entirely at the racing market.

There's many a slip . . . and nowhere more so than in horse breeding, so not all these foals reach the racecourse. Fewer than one in three actually start their careers as two-year-olds.

The principal testing time for a flat racehorse comes in his second season, when he is three. The best of each generation meet in the annual Classic races, which all have a history going back 150 years and more. There are two over a mile at Newmarket in the Spring, the One Thousand Guineas for fillies and the Two Thousand Guineas for colts; two over one and a half miles at Epsom in the summer, the Oaks for fillies and the Derby – the Blue Riband of the Turf – and then the one and three quarter mile St. Leger at Doncaster in September. These are the rich prizes (when Grundy won the Derby in 1975 he earned his owner £31,430) but now there are numerous other big rewards to be won in races which pit generation against generation, among them the King George VI and Queen Elizabeth Stakes at Ascot in July (worth £24,100 to the owner of the winner. Grundy

also won this race in 1975), the £50,000 added Benson and Hedges Gold Cup at York and the Champion Stakes at Newmarket in October.

But valuable rewards like these can go only to the relative few. Prize money for the whole of the flat racing season of 1973 totalled £4,628,889, which sounds a lot less when one considers it spread around the nearly 7,000 horses competing. In fact, the 'average loss expectation', a figure produced by measuring the amount of prize money available for each horse against its annual costs, has risen steadily in the years since the 1939–45 war – and over the last few seasons alarmingly. Statisticians reckon that an 'average loss' of £885 per horse

in 1969 had risen to no less than £1,715 per horse by 1974.

The situation would be even more bleak were it not for the considerable contribution made to racing by industry and commerce in the form of sponsorship. Money from sponsoring companies made up 15 per cent of the 1973 total, Levy Board grants provided 31 per cent and the racecourses 26 per cent. The remainder, 28 per cent, came from the owners themselves.

National Hunt Racing

So racing plainly provides no easy road to riches for the majority, but if owners on the flat consider themselves hard done by what of their opposite numbers in the other half of the racing game? For National Hunt enthusiasts the returns are much lower. In 1973 about 4,500 horses were chasing their share of the £2,091,710 prize money, the proportional contributions being sponsors 15 per cent, Levy Board 39 per cent, racecourses 10 per cent and owners 36 per cent. And in jumping there is rarely the cushion of breeding value to fall back on, since the male animals are almost without exception geldings and the mares — relatively fewer in number than on the flat — cannot command the paddock price of their flat racing sisters. The top class steeplechaser will not reach his prime until he is about nine, by which time both his sire and dam may be dead, or at any rate past the age of fecundity.

The course at Goodwood.

But National Hunt enthusiasts are accustomed to the 'poor relation' tag that has been theirs ever since the sport had its beginnings in the 18th century hunting field! Before that time all racing had been on the flat; so, to a large extent, had hunting. A new element entered the Chase with the coming of enclosures and the spread of hedges, ditches and fencing. The hunting man realized that, if he was to stay close to his hounds, then he must teach himself and his horse to jump. This, of course, proved no disadvantage; indeed, it provided hunting with what is now, for many, its greatest attraction, and the sportsman of the day became so enamoured of the hell-for-leather hunts across brook, bank and hedge that he was loath to put them aside during hunting's close season. So he began to engage in private matches with friends of like mind in which hounds and quarry played no part. The originators, so it is said, were a couple of gentlemen named O'Callaghan and Blake who, in 1752, wagered 'a hogshead of claret, a pipe of port and a quarter cask of old Jamaica rum' on the outcome of a contest to decide who had the best hunter, the winner being the first home in a two-and-a-half-mile gallop between the Co. Cork villages of Buttevant and St. Leger. The legend of that famous day speaks of a race from Buttevant Church to St. Leger Steeple; and so similar events which followed became known as steeplechases.

Their attraction was not immediately obvious to those then prompting flat racing and, though an event for hunters was occasionally included, this was, strangely, run on the flat, until at Bedford in 1811 someone had the bright idea of erecting four fences – '4ft 6in high, with a strong bar at the top' – for the horses to negotiate. This first recorded jumping race was, it seems, a disappointment, drawing only two starters.

And so it continued, for, with the notable exception of the greatest jumping race of them all, the Grand National, an attraction from its very first year, 1839, it can be said that steeplechasing took a long time to get off the ground. Somewhere along the road its development split in two, one half remaining firmly linked with the hunting field and becoming the ancestor of today's point-to-point, and the other taking the more professional fork. This latter route was anything but straight and narrow. In fact, the new sport struggled into life under the handicap of a very doubtful reputation, attracting as it did the cast-offs – human and equine – of flat racing, and lacking an overall authoritative leadership to provide both direction and discipline.

Finally, a long period in the doldrums ended with the establishment in 1866 of the National Hunt Committee, which was to do for steeplechasing what the Jockey Club has done for flat racing, and which was to remain firmly in control of its destiny until the two bodies merged in 1968.

RIGHT Jockeys in the stalls.

BELOW A string of racehorses out for early morning exercise.

Good name it may have had; poor relation it stayed. Trainers, jockeys and race promoters made some sort of living, but for owners it could never be more than a sport, when only the Grand National offered a worthwhile prize in money terms. Even the Cheltenham Gold Cup, the acknowledged level weight championship test over fences, was, practically from its inaugural year, 1924, a mere £1,000 plate – until after the last war.

The present-day situation has improved, thanks to a considerable influx of sponsorship money, which can itself be attributed in no little part to the attention that steeplechasing – indeed all forms of racing – receives from television. Sponsorship has meant a series of valuable contests, nearly all of them handicaps, stretching from October through to the end of April. These are familiar highlights in a busy calendar in which no longer need a top-flight chaser's whole programme be directed merely towards the Grand National (also sponsored nowadays) at the Liverpool spring meeting.

The increase of worthwhile prizes has resulted in a greater spread of National Hunt heroes. Previously these were almost exclusively Grand National winners; but the greatest post-war steeplechaser, Arkle, who won three Gold Cups and numerous big sponsored prizes, never ran in the Grand National; nor did his frequent rival, Mill House; nor yet did little Mandarin, who won the first running of the Hennessy Gold Cup in 1957, scored again in 1961 and then the following June wrote his name – and that of his rider, Fred Winter – indelibly into racing history with a fantastic success in the Grand Steeplechase de Paris, when he completed almost the entire course with his usual rubber bit hanging useless in his mouth after it had snapped in two at the third of the 21 fences.

But the great race over four-and-a-half miles of Aintree's unique fences – Becher's Brook, Valentine's, the Canal Turn and the rest – still exercises its almost magical attraction, and perhaps no post-war Grand National winner caught the public imagination more than Red Rum, who in 1973 overtook the gallant top weight, the Australian horse Crisp, a few strides before the post, and then in 1974 became the first since Reynoldstown (1935 and 1936) to win in two successive years. The Grand National is, of course, a handicap, and Red Rum carried only 10st 5lb when he set a new record of 9min. 1.9sec for the course in 1973, whereas Crisp was burdened with 12st. But the following year it was Red Rum's turn to shoulder top weight – and he did it with an ease that made the public wild with delight.

Many a romance is weaved about a Grand National winner. In Red Rum's case truth was almost stranger than fiction. Bred as a five-furlong sprinter – indeed, he was a winner over that distance as a two-year-old – stabled behind some second-hand car showrooms, trained on the seashore, recovered from an 'incurable' foot complaint – these are just some of the ingredients of his story.

Several of the winners of this, the world's greatest steeplechase – like Teal in 1952, Oxo in 1959 and Merryman II in 1960 – started their racing careers in point-to-points. Similarly, some Cheltenham Gold Cup heroes have sprung from this more modest sphere. Linwell (1957) was one, Woodland Venture (1967) another. The Dikler, successful in the 1973 Gold Cup and placed second to the Irish invader Captain Christy the following year, appeared for the first time over fences as a six-year-old at the Beaufort Hunt meeting in 1969, finishing second. The connection between point-to-

Beaufort Hunt meeting in 1969, finishing second. The connection between point-to-pointing and steeplechasing is strong, for in addition to providing a nursery for the budding stars, point-to-pointing can also be a haven for the old 'chaser, whose speed may have been slackened by the passing seasons, but who can still give a young owner-rider a great deal of fun in a point-to-point. Indeed he will quite probably win one into the bargain and certainly give the impression of enjoying it all himself at the same time. Retirement to some lonely field is not always the happiest of fates to await the racehorse past his usefulness on professional tracks.

Point-to-Points

There is still scope for the amateur in National Hunt racing, though the economics of life in the seventies tilt the odds heavily against any modern-day Corinthian, and recently-imposed restrictions are tending to squeeze out the non-professional trainer, the so-called permit-holder. But point-to-pointing – Hunt racing – remains a sport for the amateur, in which the majority of horses are owner-trained and most are owner-ridden.

It is based four-square on the hunting field (the Masters of Foxhounds Association was its first controlling body and is still strongly represented on the Jockey Club committee which guides its fortunes today) and the meetings – there are not far short of 200 in the

BELOW Training.

brief February to May season – are nearly all run by individual Hunts. The sport shares a common ancestry with National Hunt racing – the O'Callaghan/Blake type end of season cross-country match – and originally the races did run literally from point to point. Natural country prevailed for a long time, but 'made' courses, with 'island' fences instead of hedges, began to arrive as the emphasis shifted from a participant to a spectator sport, when Hunts realized that by attracting the public they could also ensure a much-needed income.

Nowadays the layout of courses and construction of fences to the correct dimensions are subject to scrutiny by official Jockey Club inspectors. But, though the trend is more and more towards spreading the cost burden by sharing courses – some are used three, four or even five times a season – there is still room for individuality and charm. Grandstands are normally non-existent – a suitable hillside will provide the necessary vantage points – and there are rarely any buildings. Tents and marquees afford all the shelter needed for administration, changing rooms, tote, refreshments, etc.

Travel 'shanks's pony' to a point-to-point and it is truly a free sport, for no admission charge is permissible for persons – only for vehicles. But since few Hunt racing centres, even the popular, much-used courses, are easily accessible by public transport, nearly all visitors arrive by car, paying anything from £1 to £5 for the privilege of occupying a place in one of the car-parks, from which much of the racing can be seen.

All programmes have at least five races, some six or more, all of them over at least three miles, with a minimum of 18 fences. The crowds tend to congregate by the final fence and round the finishing post – often the only part of the course where, for safety's sake, the line is marked by ropes or perhaps a chestnut paling fence – but the visitor can move almost anywhere he pleases, the only restricted zone being the parade ring.

Horses competing in point-to-points must all be hunters and have certificates to prove it, though there will be a wide variation in the amount of hunting that individual horses will have been subjected to. Usually the race with the most genuine hunters – and sadly often the smallest field – will be that for members of the promoting Hunt. Other races are staged for horses from up to eight neighbouring or adjacent Hunts. One is normally reserved for 'maidens', i.e. non-winners, and there will also be a couple of 'Open' races, which may be contested by hunters from anywhere in the country and in which competition is consequently keenest.

At some meetings the gambler will have a choice between bookmakers and tote, though over the last few years the 'machine' has been withdrawn from all fixtures where the turnover has proved uneconomic. But there will always be bookmakers with their boards and chalks to add colour to the scene. A lot of unkind things have been said and written about point-to-point bookmakers – and some of it is true. They do have their problems at the less well-patronized fixtures, where the market is weak and where a single £10 bet might be enough to unbalance their columns, but little can be said in favour of the system prevailing at some others where the bookies themselves – or perhaps more correctly the principal one – seem to have the power to exclude anyone outside their ring from setting up in business. Consequently the situation arises where four or five bookies have the field to themselves and offer prices which are virtually valueless, in the sure knowledge that there will be plenty among the once or twice a year public who will happily bet with them. At the bigger meetings, where no 'ring' operates and where there may be up to 50 boards, the punter receives a fair crack of the whip.

At most of the point-to-points one of the Open races will be confined to ladies, who are also permitted to ride against men in members' races and in adjacent Hunts' events where there is no 'maiden' or 'moderate' restriction. In ladies' only Open races the weight to be carried need only be 11st, compared with the 12st 7lb minimum of other races, and consequently they are usually run at a faster pace. The suggestion that it is because the ladies are unable to keep their mounts from running away is not only ungallant but generally false, since there are many lady riders who have proved themselves easily the equal of their male counterparts.

Open races carry the highest prize, though the rules do not allow this to be more than £40 for the winner, compared with the £30 maximum in other races. So, though the costs involved are smaller than those for racing proper, point-to-pointing can never be a money making sport for the owner. However, it is one from which a great deal of enjoyment can be extracted in return for a comparatively modest outlay; modest, that is, depending on the purchase price of that first essential – the horse. And that in itself will depend on whether an individual puts the main emphasis on a horse for hunting, with the possibility of subsequent racing, or on a horse for racing, with the necessity, in order to be eligible, of preparatory hunting. Some animals fill both roles with equal ease, but an owner planning a serious racing programme usually arranges for his horse's hunting to be finished by Christmas so that preparation for point-to-points can then begin.

For the novice rider the point-to-point can be the first step up a long ladder. Several of today's leading professionals started out as raw recruits in this amateur game. And for the novice rider's mount there can be no better choice than a horse who has already had plenty of racing experience. He need not necessarily be in the veteran category, but will be on offer at a lower price if he is and, though his race expectation may not be high, he will usually possess that desirable 'safe jumper'

accolade. Years of galloping round all sorts of courses with all sorts of riders will have taught him how to keep out of trouble and will have given him that priceless 'extra leg' to help retain his equilibrium after a blunder that would send a youngster sprawling. A horse aged six or seven who has already won over hurdles or fences is even more desirable . . . but his price-tag is likely to be well beyond the pocket of someone on the lookout for a point-to-pointer; if, on the other hand, he is six or seven with no worthwhile form, and perhaps has fallen a few times over National Hunt fences, the price may be right but he is better left alone, at least by the inexperienced. Similarly, the newcomer should steer clear of the young, untried horse – a novice can't learn much from another novice.

The ideal would be an eight- or nine-year-old with proven ability to get round over fences or hurdles, not necessarily a winner (indeed, a non-winner could be an advantage since there would still be scope in maiden races) and up to his rider's weight, not just racing weight but hunting weight too, which could be about a stone more and need to be carried for a lot longer.

A study of the prospect's past record can pay excellent dividends later when it comes to deciding racecourse tactics, but it is also essential initially to glean such information as whether he acts on heavy or hard ground (paragons can manage both but paragons are rare) and whether his racecourse career has been peppered with lengthy absences which might suggest the leg troubles to which horses are so prone. 'Firing' – the operation designed to repair broken-down limbs – should be fairly obvious and, while hardly a recommendation, need not be a major stumbling block, particularly if the operation is an old one and the horse has subsequently raced extensively. Yes, study of the form-book will reveal much – but a few minutes in the company of an experienced jockey who has ridden the horse in some of his races will tell even more.

RIGHT Head of a ten-year-old chestnut gelding which has had a good career as a hunter and as a point-to-point winner.

Horse and Pony Breeding

JANE KIDD

RIGHT The Lusitano is indigenous to Portugal. They were used as Cavalry mounts. They still do light agricultural work and are sometimes trained for the bullring.

BELOW A herd of quality German Horses.

The United Kingdom's great contribution to horse breeding was the development of the Thoroughbred, the fastest and most valuable horse in the world. It was Charles II who provided much of the impetus for this development. He promoted racing, after lifting the ban imposed on the sport by Cromwell. He encouraged improvements to Britain's racehorse, which at the time of his Restoration was the now extinct Galloway Pony. In particular, refined Eastern blood was imported to cross with this tough small British racing stock. Between 1660 and 1760 more than two hundred Arabs, Turks and Barbs came into the country. The most important of these were the three Arab stallions, Darley Arabian, Byerley Turk and Godolphin Arabian, to whom all British Thoroughbreds can be traced.

The first great racehorse, Flying Childers, was born in 1715, but at this time the average size of stock was little more than 14·2hh. Over the next 150 years enormous improvements

were made by use of systematic breeding methods and favourable environmental conditions (feed and climate). By the middle of the last century the breed of Thoroughbred as we know it today had been established. Since then its function, racing, has expanded into a major worldwide industry. Other countries have tried to develop their own breed of racehorse but none succeeded so British Thoroughbreds are the foundation of racing stock all over the world. They have also been used as a means of injecting 'class' and speed into many other breeds.

The Arab, too, has played a major role in the foundation and improvement of other breeds. It has been doing so for much longer, as it is the oldest pure breed in the world. According to legend the Arabs bred wild in the Yemen until 3,000 BC when one was caught and tamed by Baz, the great great grandson of Noah. After their contribution towards the foundation of the Thoroughbred they were rarely seen in the United Kingdom until the end of the last century. Mr and Mrs Blunt bought some from the tribes of the Arabian desert and took them back to the Crabbet Park Stud in Sussex. By 1909, 96 stallions stood there. This awakened interest in the breed. The Arab quickly acquired supporters in Britain. Some wanted them just to look at; they are such decorative horses. Others used them for riding as they are gay with powers of endurance, but probably most are used for pure and cross bred breeding.

The Arab and the Thoroughbred have been the most influential and famous of breeding stock in the United Kingdom, but there are many more intriguing types. Some of Britain's oldest breeds, the native ponies, graze on the moors and hills where the grass is scarce and the land of poor agricultural value. The nature of this terrain and the manner in which the herds lived have varied from area to area, so

ABOVE A Shetland pony.

BELOW The great Irish Draught horse is a sound and solid animal which is much crossed with Thoroughbreds to produce the renowned Irish hunter.

ABOVE Shandy, a fourteen-year-old Welsh Cob and prize winner pulls a Stanhope gig driven by Mrs Marylian Watney at the Brockenhurst show. Shandy was an ex-costermonger's horse and was trained to play a part in Steptoe and Son, the successful television serial. The Welsh Cob is crossed extensively with Thoroughbreds and light hunters to make versatile family horses and it is also becoming one of the most successful types in Combined Driving. This is a sport similar to the Event competitions held for riding horses and involves presentation, dressage and cross-country work.

that nine distinctive types have emerged. Each of these has now established its own stud book. In the north there are the largest and sturdiest ponies, the Highland, Dale and Fell. However, the most northern breed of all, the Shetland, is also the smallest, standing between 26in and 42in high. The three southern breeds, the Exmoor with its mealy muzzle, the Dartmoor and the New Forest are finer ponies. The first two are not more than 12·3hh, but the New Forest can grow to 14·2hh.

Westwards, the Welsh mountain ponies, have roamed the Welsh hills for centuries and are noted for their quality and agility. They have been used as foundation stock for many breeds, including, it has been said, the Thoroughbred. Finally, in the south west of Ireland is the country of the Connemara, an ancient breed which shows the influence of the addition of Andalusian and Arab blood. They thrive on poor keep but grow larger when well fed. The show jumper Dundrum and the eventer Eagle Rock have Connemara heritage.

In sharp contrast to the native pony is the Heavy Horse. In mediaeval times these were bred as chargers to carry knights in armour into battle. Later they became the main source of power for the farmer. In England there are three main types, differentiated like the ponies according to the area. In Scotland in the Clyde Valley the Clydesdale is bred, famous for its feathery legs and high stepping action. In the Midlands is to be found the heaviest of them

all, the Shire. Further south, the chestnut Suffolk Punch is the only type without those handsome feathery legs. However, the heavy horse of greatest value in today's equestrian activities is the Irish Draught. Originating from the Connemara it is not so large as the English Heavy Horses. Crossed with the Thoroughbred it has been the basis of the Irish Hunter stock.

An English indigenous breed too light to be Heavy Horse is the Cleveland Bay. Bred in the north east of Yorkshire it is an all purpose horse which has been used for more than two hundred years for light farm work, pulling carriages and riding. Another versatile horse is the more active but smaller Welsh Cob. Bred in Cardigan and Pembrokeshire, it has been used for many years as a family horse. Today it is becoming one of the most successful types in Combined Driving – George Bowman's team of greys were members of Britain's victorious 1974 world champion team. However, the most popular driving horse with the crowds is the Hackney. This breed of exceptionally fast, spectacular trotters used to be the means of speedy travel for the East Anglian farmers during the seventeenth, eighteenth and nineteenth centuries. Now their main activity is to show off their paces and conformation in classes confined to the breed, held at all the major shows.

Such are the breeds of England which originated from a mixture of stock but now breed true to type. Stud books are kept for all

of them so that ancestors can be traced. However, these types do not fulfil all the needs of the modern equestrian world. The majority of today's horse-minded people hunt, show, event, show jump or do dressage. For these purposes the occasional Thoroughbred might be suitable, but good ones are difficult to find, for the best are kept in the more remunerative racing world. The cross bred is the most popular horse for hunting and competitive riding. For these there are no stud books but with the exception of the Field Hunter, the conformation and character of the horses needed for these competitions can be clearly defined.

The Field Hunter, on the other hand, covers a great variety of types; practically any type which is sound can find a home as a hunter. The rotund Welsh farmer would be happy with a Welsh Cob whereas a heavy gentleman in Leicestershire would prefer a large up to weight Thoroughbred. Every possible type of horse has been used at one time or another to go hunting.

The horses that compete in show classes must, above all, have excellent conformation (this is outlined later). The Hack should be an elegant creature. It originated from the animals that the nobility used to show off on. During the last century and before they were used for socializing exercises in such smart areas as Rotten Row. They are still expected to be well trained, to look pretty and to behave beautifully.

ABOVE The Cleveland Bay.
This is a popular old English
breed and the only native
horse that was not a Heavy
Horse. It has excellent
hunter qualities with plenty
of stamina and a natural
tendency to jump. Notice its
long back and unpronounced
withers. It has been much
cross-bred with
Thoroughbreds to produce
Hunters and lighter carriage
horses.

RIGHT The Anglo-Arab
combines the qualities of the
Thoroughbred and the Arab
and as such can often be a
superlatively good riding
horse. Anglo-Arabs have been
extensively bred in France.

RIGHT Hunting in the New
Forest. It is important to suit
the horse to the country over
which he will be hunting.

The Show Hack is either Small (under 15hh.)
or Large (15hh. to 15·3hh.). They tend to be a
cross between ponies and Thoroughbreds,
Arabs or Anglo-Arabs, although the odd pure
Thoroughbred is successful.

The Show Hunter should be a tougher type
of horse. Although usually too valuable to be
tested, their purpose is to carry their rider over
all types of country for anything up to five
hours at a time. For this they need to be a
comfortable ride, have good paces and indicate
in their conformation that they are sound,
strong animals. As a Hunter suitable to carry a
young girl must have different dimensions from
one for a heavy man, the classes are divided.
There are classes for Light, Medium and Heavy
weights, as well as for the Small Hunter (under
15·2hh.). The typical method of breeding a
hunter is to cross a Thoroughbred with a
heavier mare (Irish Draught, Cleveland, Welsh
Cob or Half Bred).

The horses for competitive sports used to be
rather like Field Hunters as they came in all
shapes and sizes. Horses that jumped high
fences included such types as cobs, hackneys,
Thoroughbreds and ponies. Today a more
uniform type is emerging; the general demand
is for a horse with the 'class' and ability of
the Thoroughbred, combined with the sensible
temperament and substance usually associated
with heavier breeds. Such a horse's athletic
ability can be harnessed to jump fences and
perform dressage movements as well as gallop.

Within this general outline the emphasis in
each of the three competitive disciplines is on
different characteristics. In eventing the
premium is on endurance and boldness; in
jumping, a quick thinking careful horse with
great gymnastic ability is needed; and in
dressage a co-operative temperament and
straight spectacular movement are sought.
Consequently, just as racehorse breeders vary
the blood according to whether they want a
sprinter, classic horse, stayer or National
Hunt horse, so do competition breeders. Those
concentrating on eventers use more
Thoroughbred blood; those on jumpers, native
breeds to inject the 'cunning'; and those
concentrating on dressage horses usually find
some continental blood is best for movement
and temperament.

Principles of Breeding

The Breeder's primary consideration is to have clear aims. The first, that one and all should have, is to breed a sound animal. This means that the parents must not suffer from hereditary defects. The most seriously defective are those horses not clear in the wind, that roar or whistle, those with eyes showing cataracts, or those whose legs have sidebones or bone spavins.

The conformation or shape of a horse is an important indication of whether or not it will remain sound. So a well proportioned horse is not only more pleasant to look at, but also more likely to stand up to work. However, a horse showing weaknesses in conformation need not be discarded for breeding purposes, as for hereditary unsoundness, but can be simply mated with a partner who has the shape to offset the problem. Thus a mare with a short neck and little front should be put to a stallion with a long neck and a good front.

Although the conformation varies from breed to breed, the general outline of a horse likely to stay sound is much the same. The back should be gently curved, as one that is convex or too hollow is weak. The hindquarters should be powerful and rounded, the hock strong and the hind leg not too straight or too curved, for it is from the hind end the power is derived. The ribs should be well sprung and have depth (i.e. requires a large girth). The shoulder (except for carriage horses) should be sloping and the neck convex and of good length. A pretty, bold head with large eyes set well apart is attractive and indicative of a good temperament. The legs should be placed squarely, the forelegs not too close together, the knees flat, the cannon bone short and flat, and the joints not rounded or brittle. The pasterns should not be too long or upright and the hooves must be rounded and open.

The next aim for the breeder is to build up a clear picture of the type of produce needed.

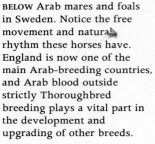

BELOW Arab mares and foals in Sweden. Notice the free movement and natural rhythm these horses have. England is now one of the main Arab-breeding countries, and Arab blood outside strictly Thoroughbred breeding plays a vital part in the development and upgrading of other breeds.

Once they have decided upon the work they want their produce for (racing, jumping, farming, etc.), they must establish what characteristics are needed in order to perform the work well, such as the most suitable shape, temperament and specific ability. Then they can start the interesting part, the selection of parents.

This selection is based on three sources of information. Firstly, the appearance of the parents. A powerful hindquarter and second thigh indicate the ability to jump; and a round generous eye indicates a good temperament. A seasoned horseman develops an 'eye for a horse', and can pick out one which has the qualities needed to perform a job. Nevertheless, even experts have been misled by outward appearance. The horse's ability can really only be judged by actually testing him at the task. Performance records as well as knowledge of the conformation are needed to paint a fuller picture of the prospective parents. However these are poor indications of genetic make up. A parent can pass on characteristics not apparent in him. A small mare can produce an enormous foal. Consequently, information is needed about the ancestors' conformation and performances. Only by analysing pedigrees, performance records and conformation can a breeder hope to influence the shape and ability of produce. He cannot calculate how to breed a Derby winner or an Olympic Medal horse, but he can raise the standard and suitability of the stock by these systematic rather than haphazard breeding methods.

Today's horses are bred mainly for five purposes. Firstly, to maintain a pure breed of horse, such as the Arab, when the breeder's aim is to produce the best possible type according to the definition of the breed. Secondly, to race, when the central aim is speed combined with varying degrees of endurance. Thirdly, for children to ride, when size and temperament are most important; conformation and athletic ability are less to be considered. Fourthly, to go

RIGHT A Show hack. The conformation of a horse is important not only for appearances but also because a well-made horse will move well and is less likely to suffer from strains. This horse is a superb example of what to look for. The head is elegant, and well set onto the neck, the shoulder is sloped, allowing for free movement of the forelegs. The horse is deep through the girth so there is plenty of room for the heart and lungs. The back is short and strong, the legs straight and clean, and the quarters rounded and strong.

RIGHT These two Welsh Cobs show what a difference conformation can make to the quality of a horse. Looking at the Cob on the left, notice particularly the slope of the shoulders, the delicacy of the head and the way it is set onto the neck, and the sweeping line through the quarters into the hind legs. Then compare it with the Cob on the right, which is a Welsh pony section D.

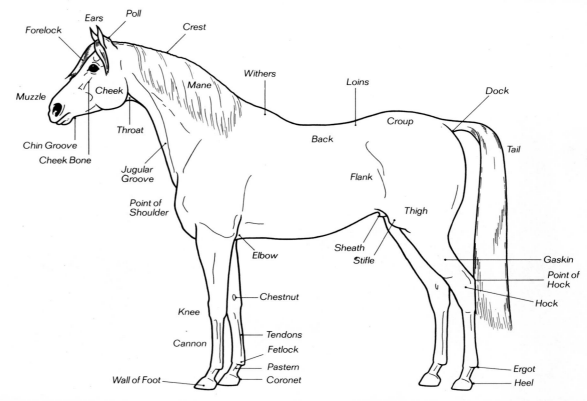

133

Steeplechasers and flat racers.

active. In 1918 The Arab Horse Society was formed. Pure bred and part bred Stud Books were started, shows encouraged to hold classes for the breed (now more than fifty run Arab events) and mares offered premiums. There are nearly 200 studs producing Arab horses, and since there are more of this breed in England than in any other country in the world except the United States, international buyers come here to acquire additional or foundation Arab stock.

Breeding Racehorses

The most systematic breeders are those of racehorses. The returns from a successful racehorse are so high in terms of money, prestige and pleasure that vast amounts of capital and thought have gone into this form of breeding. In the United Kingdom and Ireland there are about 7,000 Thoroughbred breeders. Ninety per cent have three mares or fewer and only ten have more than thirty. About half are commercial breeders selling their yearlings (2,345 in 1970) mainly at the Newmarket, Doncaster and Dublin autumn sales. Most of the remainder are rich, private people hoping to produce their classic winner.

Within the Thoroughbred breeding system there are four types of produce, requiring different types of mating. There is the quick-maturing offspring likely to win as a two-year-old and over sprint distances from then onwards. Then there is the classic horse bred to run in the prestige races of one and a half

hunting, when toughness, soundness and boldness are most important. Finally, for competitive riding, for which the most important feature is athletic ability combined with a temperament that allows the rider to make use of this asset.

Breeding Pure Breds

Many British breeders aim to produce stock showing the best possible characteristics of that type rather than to perform a particular job of work. For the more flourishing breeds there are show classes at major events. Breeders of pure breds include those of native ponies, Heavy Horses and the Cleveland Bay. The breeders of Arabs are amongst the most numerous and

miles. Thirdly, there is the slower-maturing stayer, for whom stamina plays as important a part as speed. Finally, there is the National Hunt horse who needs jumping ability as well as stamina and speed.

Most of the breeders in this country are involved in producing the first category. The returns are quicker. The produce are on the racecourse at an earlier age and, it is to be hoped, winning. However, it is the second category on which most money is spent. A stallion likely to sire this type of animal is an expensive mate. Owners can only get approved mares to him. Nor do they pay a straight fee. They have to obtain a nomination to him or they have to buy shares in him.

The breeding of stayers is not as popular in the United Kingdom as in France. The longer time taken to prove themselves and earn money makes them less commercial. The National Hunt horses need even more patient breeders. The hurdlers have often raced on the flat, or are of that type, but the chasers need a different ancestry and characteristics. They have to race for two to four miles over jumps about four and a half feet high. Many do not see a racecourse before they are five, and may not reach their prime until close to nine years of age.

The breeding of chasers is rarely done at smart studs with large quantities of mares. The mainstay of this production has been the Irish farmer. In shabby farms all over Ireland,

handsome expensive youngsters are produced. These colourful Irish farmers run the odd mare with the cattle. They put them to stallions with jumping and staying blood, whose fees are rarely as much as £200. But these farmers know their horses, their abilities and their pedigrees. They can reel off the fortunes of the ancestors just as smartly as the efficient stud director at a flat race stud.

Breeding Ponies

Ponies have been bred in England since prehistoric times. Each of the nine native types now has its own stud book and under the auspices of the Ponies of Britain Society (founded in 1952), breeding, competitions, and demand for them have been nurtured. The Welsh are particularly popular and are numerically the strongest with 478 stallions at the beginning of the seventies. In the past, these breeds of native pony have been the foundation stock for most of our horses; today they are the foundation stock for the children's riding pony. Crossed with the Thoroughbred or Arab these native ponies gain the class and the ability needed for jumping, showing, eventing and the like.

The Welsh has been the most popular cross. One famous Welsh mare was Welsh Gypsy Gold who, when covered by the Arab Naseel, was the mother of six winners in the show ring, including Pretty Polly and My Pretty Maid.

Breeding Hunters

The breeders of hunters practise haphazard methods of breeding. It would be difficult for them to do otherwise for there is no type cast hunter to aim for. They can be any shape, size or colour. A breeder can produce practically any type of animal and it will have a use somewhere. The other reason for the haphazard system is that a hunter does not fetch a great price. Producing them is rarely a commercial business. Most of the breeders are owners of old mares that they have hunted, and usually they do not seek out the most complimentary mate but simply the nearest and cheapest stallion.

The Hunter Improvement Society was formed

RIGHT Pony stallions lined up at the Ascot Stallion Show. The Hunter Improvement Society scheme is still operating successfully in Britain and ensures that good Thoroughbred stallions are placed strategically all over the country, where they are available at low prices to local mares. Although the stallions have got pedigrees they are judged upon their conformation and soundness, not on past performance or their ancestors.

BELOW A cob.

in 1885 to promote the breeding of horses at a time when England was importing large quantities of them. It does much to ensure that this diversified, often indiscriminate large group of breeders do produce the best animal possible under the circumstances. They award between sixty and seventy premiums to sound, good looking stallions annually. Each is a subsidy of up to £500 in return for which the owner has to stand his stallion at a low standard fee (£20 to members in 1975). Consequently, good stallions are within the price range of lowly mare owners. In addition the Society offers premiums to mares with a foal by their stallions. At Affiliated shows, the best looking mares are awarded £15.

The Society favours mares with bone and substance. Their premium stallions are all Thoroughbreds, so in order to obtain the good sense and toughness of a hunter, a heavier mare is needed. Such mares are increasingly difficult to find as the work horses disappear. Originally, the mainstay was the Irish Draught mare, but supply is dwindling. The Cleveland Bay is a British breed that can add the substance and temperament to the Thoroughbred ability. Interest in this type is increasing and the twenty odd pure bred stallions in this country are receiving growing numbers of mares.

Breeding Competition Horses

Competitions have become a feature of modern equestrian life. They have, of course, been held

for centuries but not on the scale of today. Over the last decade new riders have been recruited to the equestrian world at a high rate and whatever their standard there are appropriate competitions. The standard and range of events have increased so much that children and riding club members, as well as international riders, can compete in show jumping, eventing, dressage, hunter trials and long distance rides. The pure bred horse suits few of these. The Arab shines as a horse to ride for long distances, but has rarely the courage or size for competitions. The Welsh Cob and Cleveland might play a minor role, but they have not the 'class' or activity for high grade work. The Thoroughbred can be a great Event horse, but his temperamental, excitable ways means that often only the best horseman can handle him. The demand today is for a horse with a large quantity of that great English Thoroughbred blood tempered with the good sense of less refined breeds. Riders want a horse with the 'class' to jump, gallop and be a good ride, yet the temperament to cope with their work in a sensible manner.

In Britain we have no pure breed suitable to meet these needs so we must cross those that exist. This approach has been used to produce the Hunter for more than 150 years but without adopting systematic methods or making any attempts to establish a uniform type. This is not the case in Europe, where they, too, are experiencing the same booming demand for competition horses. They, like us in Britain, have met this demand with cross breds, but in an entirely different manner. They have bred them in the same way as for pure breds, i.e. as Thoroughbreds. They have kept up stud books for them, recorded pedigrees and in most countries tested both parents' ability, not on the racecourse, but in areas where the horses can show the skills for which they are being bred: over cross-country courses, show jumps and in dressage arenas.

In Europe these systematic methods of breeding competition horses have been helped by the prominent role played by governments. In most countries they have realised both the prestige value of breeding their own competition horses and the economic benefits of not having to import their equestrian resources.

The Swedish government was one of the first to play a direct role in breeding riding horses. At the end of the last century it started a stud book for the Swedish Half Bred, and financed two studs at Flyinge and Stronsholm. The Swedish Half Bred has become one of the most successful competition horses in the world. They have won Olympic gold medals in dressage, eventing and show jumping. Many of the Germans prefer them to their own breeds for dressage (Liselotte Linsenhoff's Piaff, the individual Gold Medal Winner for Germany at the 1972 Olympics, was a Swedish horse).

The Swedish Half Bred is not a pure breed. The authorities' aim is to produce horses with

BELOW A Swiss-bred chestnut mare whose sire was a Polish Arab and whose dam was of French saddle horse blood. The foal's sire was a Swedish Half Bred. It is important in any breeding plan to find a stallion whose points, both good and bad, complement those of the mare.

Large numbers of horses are bred on the plains of Hungary and are looked after by the Scikos herdsmen.

good temperaments and conformation, who move well and show athletic ability. In order to achieve this the Swedes often bring in international blood to eradicate any weaknesses exposed in their horses. Thus Hanoverians, Trakehners and Thoroughbreds are brought from Germany and England as the need arises. The only stipulations are firstly, that all stock is pedigree and secondly, that they pass performance tests. At the National Stud of Flyinge in the south of Sweden the stallions take these tests in their third year. They have a road walk of 12–15km at a minimum speed of 240 metres per minute, followed by a 3·5km cross country course of 14 obstacles at a maximum height of one metre and width of two metres. A minimum speed of 450 metres per minute must be maintained. Finally, they have a flat race of 1,200 metres when they must go at more than 700 metres per minute. On completion they are subjected to a veterinary

examination. Those who do not pass this rigid test of stamina, soundness and temperament are not allowed to breed. And those who do are still not given a final 'all clear' until their foals have been examined.

Even having passed these tests the 40 odd stallions at Flyinge are under continual surveillance. Displays of bad temper or poor feeding result in gelding. They are all ridden and driven throughout the autumn and winter, which helps to discover the scope and depth of their ability. Stallions performing Grand Prix movements are common sights on visits to the Stud. One of the most successful sires, Gaspari, actually represented Sweden in two Olympic dressage events.

The Swedes have laid greatest importance on temperament and athletic ability. With their systematic methods of breeding, analysing pedigrees and testing of sires, they have shown that it is possible to produce those characteristics. Their Half Bred has become renowned for its intelligent temperament and excellent movement.

The Germans have placed their emphasis on power and a temperament that will be prepared to take discipline rather than think independently. The breeding of horses with such features has not been controlled by the central government but by regional associations, usually supported by provincial governments. Thus there are more than 12 breeds of riding horse in Germany, for example, the Bavarian horse in Bavaria, the Hanoverian around Hanover and the Holstein in Schleswig Holstein. Except for the Trakehner, the breeds are purely defined by birthplace. Thus a foal with Holstein parents born in the district of Hanover is entered in the Hanoverian stud book as a Hanoverian. As a result, the breeds are becoming less and less distinctive and a German Riding Horse is emerging.

The various breeding associations, like the Swedes, keep strict controls on their breeds. Stud books have been kept for hundreds of years and although Thoroughbreds, Arabs and other pure breds are often used for upgrading, a horse without a pedigree is not used for breeding. The Germans, too, will not allow their stallions to stand merely on a basis of good pedigree and conformation. They must pass performance tests laid down by the breed's association. The Hanoverian, for instance, has to pull carriages, perform dressage tests, show jump and go across country. Mare owners can examine the results of the stallions' tests and choose the horse most likely to offset their mares' weaknesses and complement her good points.

BELOW LEFT A Trakehner stallion. These horses are still bred in private studs in West Germany. They are capable of great endurance and are good performers in all mounted sports.

BELOW The Hanoverian. This breed was originally used for light agricultural work, as a coach horse, and an artillery horse as well as a saddle horse and even a race horse. Recently breeders have concentrated on producing a lighter more elegant saddle horse. The Hanoverian has an exceptional movement and temperament which makes it one of the best competition horses in the world.

140

The French government's control over breeding is more comprehensive than any other western country. It owns nearly all the stallions in the country, whether they are used to produce horses for racing, agriculture, pleasure, competitions or meat. The French competition horse is known as the Selle Français. This is a new title for, like the Germans, the half breds used to be differentiated regionally. Now all half breds, such as the Anglo Norman, come under this one title.

The Selle Français is the result of crosses between the indigenous work mares and the pure breds such as Arabs, Thoroughbreds and trotters. Most are characterized by the influence of considerable Arab blood. This makes them more flamboyant and less amenable to discipline than the German horse.

The French base their breeding system upon conformation and pedigree. The latter is very important and the import of non pedigree English and Irish mares for breeding is discouraged by the authorities. In fact, unlike the Swedes and Germans, the French are happy with their national equestrian blood, of which they can trace the ancestry back to the time of Louis XIV. They do not believe infusions of international blood will help them to produce a better competition horse, but then they do have the largest horse population of any country in Europe.

Other countries are realising the benefits of breeding competition horses on the same lines as racehorses. Switzerland has been buying pedigree Swedish, German, French and English Thoroughbreds to stock up her National Stud, and now any of the stallions standing is made to undergo rigorous performance tests. The Swiss riding horse is in the pioneer stages and is only just old enough to start competing.

Denmark is another country which has

started to control breeding. For the last ten years the Danish Sportshorse Breeding Association has laid down qualifications for standing horses. Like the Swiss, the Danes have imported foreign pedigree breeds and subjected them to performance as well as veterinary and conformation tests. However, in Denmark the administration of breeding is in private hands. There is no government assistance. The stallions stand at private studs, mostly in Jutland.

The results of these individual efforts have been most worthwhile and the Germans and Dutch are buying large numbers of the Danish Sportshorse.

In the United Kingdom this nationally organized systematic approach to breeding competition horses does not exist. The competition horse is not yet looked upon as a type to be bred by the same systematic methods as a racehorse. There is no association for the promotion and control of this form of breeding. The majority of horses used in competitions were bred for another purpose, and it is usually only by chance that the assets needed for competition work emerged – some racehorses and hunters have proved to be great competition horses.

Nevertheless, it seems likely that more could be produced if the country specifically set out to do so. Neither of these two types were bred with primary considerations of a competition horse in mind: temperament, athletic ability, movement and power. For the Thoroughbred the most important point is speed and/or stamina, while for the hunter the main points are toughness, soundness and good conformation.

Some breeders are beginning to breed specifically competition horses through the hunter system. Many with retired successful competition mares send them to Hunter Improvement Society Premium sires. However the basis of selection is not the equal of the continentals'. The mare might have her performance record and soundness, but generally as a successful competition horse, she is cross bred. Cross breds have no pedigrees, so the ancestors cannot be analysed. The stallion will have a pedigree and usually performance records on the racecourse, but if he is a Premium sire he will have been chosen not because of these, but simply on account of his conformation and soundness. This is a system devised to produce Hunters when outward appearance is a sufficient basis for selection. Although not the ideal means of producing competition horses, these Premium sires have produced such great ones as the Olympic medal winners Psalm (silver in show jumping) and Laurieston (gold in eventing).

Outside the Hunter Improvement Society scheme increasing numbers of stallions are standing which are particularly suitable as competition sires. The reason for this is that either they themselves have proved their ability and temperament by competing, or their pedigrees show competition producing stock. Mrs. Jennie Loriston Clarke's Xenacles comes into the former category. This international dressage rider has upgraded her stallion to the advanced stage of both eventing and dressage. His progeny are equally successful, winning in both fields. Another successful producer of competition horses is King's Rhapsody, an example of the second category. Vivien Boone rode him into Grade A as a show jumper, and his progeny included the top Grade A's Rythem and Halcyon IV. King's Rhapsody is not a Thoroughbred but a cross between two pure breds, King's Counsel, a Thoroughbred, and Hoodoo, a large Hackney mare.

Other studs specifically setting out to breed competition horses have imported proven

pedigree competition blood. The Masserella family, who have owned so many top show jumpers, have two Hanoverians, Grande II and Ferdi. In Surrey at the Maple Stud stand Maple Duellist, brought over from Hanover twelve years ago, and his son Maple Duel. Maple Duellist has produced international jumpers, dressage and event winners. The Trakehner is another popular German horse, and Mr. and Mrs. Lorch of Fulmer, Bucks, are meeting increasing demand with their stallion Muschamp Danube, while Sue Falkner in Sussex won the Novice National Dressage Championship on her stallion The Black Knight whose dam is a Russian Trakehner.

These are pioneers in England. They are experimenting with a new aim in breeding, a competition horse. They have no specific Society to help them and there is no system of registration for their produce. Unlike in Europe, even a cross bred resulting from parents of established breeds has no pedigree status. This makes it difficult to discover good bloodlines of competition horses and to develop a long term breeding policy. However, in the United Kingdom, most new ideas arise from individual efforts rather than government direction. The number of individuals systematically breeding horses suitable for competitions is snowballing. They are likely soon to prove the existence of a breed in its early stages of development – the British Competition Horse.

FAR RIGHT A 'white' flat race at St. Moritz, Switzerland.

The Breeds

ELWYN HARTLEY EDWARDS

The early horse developed according to the environment in which it lived and the modern horse, in all its enormous variety, can almost certainly be traced to three basic types which emerged as a result of horses inhabiting areas distinctive in terrain and climate. The three prehistoric types were the Steppe, the Forest and the Plateau horses. The first of these has survived virtually unchanged, due possibly to the inaccessibility of its habitat. The Asiatic Wild Horse of Mongolia, *equus Przewalskii Przewalskii Poliakov,* was discovered on the Mongolian steppes by Colonel N. M. Przewalski in 1881. This primitive horse is now nearly extinct on the western edges of the Gobi desert where it was first observed by the intrepid Colonel but it is now preserved in zoos.

The Forest horse, heavier and more slow-moving than the Steppe, was the forefather of the 'cold-blood' horse, exemplified by the modern 'heavy' horse breeds of today. The Plateau horse, on the other hand, was almost the exact opposite of the Forest. It was of a finer and lighter build than the Steppe, with longer, more slender limbs and with feet of a form halfway between those of the other two primitive contemporaries, avoiding both the extreme length and narrowness of the Steppe hoof, and the broad, soup-plate proportions of that of the Forest horse.

It is a reasonable assumption that the light horses and ponies of today are the descendants of the Steppe type of horse. The original Steppe type is represented today by the Tarpan, which is still preserved in Poland.

There would probably have been a certain amount of intermingling and thus some variation of the three types but they must, in essence, be regarded as the raw material from which the modern horse and pony has evolved.

The process of evolution and improvement by natural selection has been going on ever since the days of *Eohippus,* the earliest known ancestor of the horse, but the existence of the hundreds of types of horses and ponies which make up the world equine population today is due, largely, to the influence exerted by man. In many instances environment is still a major factor in the establishment and maintenance of type and character but since the domestication of the horse some 4000 years ago, human interference by selective breeding and artificial feeding etc., has played an increasingly large role in the development of the modern horse. Bigger, stronger and faster animals have long been bred with the object of producing a type best suited to a particular purpose, though the establishment of specific breeds, of which there are now more than 200, and the introduction of recorded pedigrees, are relatively recent developments.

A 'breed', as distinct from a 'type', can be defined as a horse or pony which has been bred over a fairly long period of time and which, as a result, consistently produces stock that has clearly fixed characteristics of height, colour, appearance and action. Such horses will be the produce of 'pure-bred' parents whose pedigrees will be recorded in the Stud Book operated by their governing body and they, in turn, will be eligible for registration. The Arabian horse is a breed, for instance, as is the Thoroughbred or the Welsh pony. These horses have distinctive and immediately recognizable features and characteristics which are reproduced from one generation to the next. All three are registered in Stud Books and it is possible to trace back the breeding of any one for many generations.

Examples of types of horses would be the hunter and the Palomino. The latter, it is true, has a common coat colour of a golden shade accompanied by a white mane and tail, but these features can be obtained by the mating of parents whose colours may be likely to result in a golden-coated offspring i.e. a chestnut and a cream will probably give the required colour. Otherwise there is no uniformity of height about the Palomino or any notable characteristic of conformation. Palomino colouring can appear in a small pony or a full-size horse; some may be cobs, or short-legged, stocky individuals, while others may display something of the quality of an Arabian or a Thoroughbred. A hunter, similarly, is often the result of cross-breeding. Many are by Thoroughbred sires out of very ordinary mares of unknown ancestry, themselves the results of a number of cross matches. Some will have a percentage of 'heavy' blood in their veins, while others will have a proportion of native pony blood, such as Connemara, Highland or New Forest.

calm down the hot Thoroughbred temperament and to give the superb agility and 'cow sense' for which the Quarter Horse is famed.

By far the most popular breed in the United States, it is also established in many other countries, principally Australia, Canada, South Africa, Mexico and Central and South America.

Although the Quarter Horse was formally recognized as a breed only in 1941, the first famous progenitor of the breed was recorded in the middle of the eighteenth century. This was the Thoroughbred stallion Janus, a grandson of the Godolphin Barb, and imported to America in 1756. Today his name is listed as head of nine of the 24 main families of the breed.

The Quarter Horse is between 14·3 and 15·1hh. and weighs 1,100 to 1,300lb. A good example of the very attractive-looking breed should have a short head with a small muzzle, sharp 'foxy' ears, a well-developed jaw and

plenty of width across the forehead. His neck should be of medium length, reasonably light without being thin, and certainly not heavily crested, and it should join the shoulder at an angle of about 45 degrees. A Quarter Horse's shoulders should also slope at about 45 degrees to ensure smooth paces and the chest should be wide and deep, with plenty of heart-room. A short back is linked to broad, extremely powerful quarters, which are often steeply sloped, thus able to give added power for very fast starts. The forelegs should be heavily muscled and, in the hindlegs, thighs and gaskins must be packed with muscle.

There are two basic types of Quarter Horse: the more refined racing type, which may often be by a Thoroughbred of the right stamp from a Quarter Horse mare, and the 'bulldog' type – short-backed, rather short-legged and square, and very muscular – which is the working cowman's ideal mount.

The Quarter Horse excels in all forms of western riding and is often a star in his own right in rodeo events such as roping, reining, cutting and barrel racing. He is a great favourite of Western trail riders, of course, and is being increasingly used in non-Western activities, such as jumping, polo, and even working hunter classes at shows.

The Quarter Horse has also played a large part in bringing the other famous Western breeds to their present level of prominence and popularity. He has provided the solid basis of excellent cow horse conformation for the Paint, Pinto, Palomino and Appaloosa horses, which are essentially colour breeds. The very distinctive spotted Appaloosa Horse was originally bred by the Nez Percé Indians and skilful addition of Quarter Horse blood has developed the best specimens into eye-catching stock horses with performance to match their visual appeal.

Another highly popular made-in-America breed is the Morgan, which got its start in the east – in Springfield, Massachusetts – in 1789 with the birth of a small bay colt. Figure, who came into the hands of Vermont schoolmaster Justin Morgan, in 1793, in payment of a debt, soon began to win fame with his success in racing, pulling contests and trotting competitions. Becoming known by his owner's name, Justin Morgan then founded a whole new breed in his own lifetime!

Owing to his incredible prepotency as a sire, a large number of his foals, even from indifferent mares, inherited his compact, well-balanced, robust yet refined conformation, along with his strength, speed, amenable temperament and game spirit. Just where the unbelievable combination of genes that put him aloft as a wholly exceptional sire came from remains something of a mystery: his dam's breeding is not recorded, but it is believed that his sire was the racehorse True Briton, by Traveller, imported from England.

Today Morgans are mainly bay, and are between 14 and 15hh. The breed's build is robust yet refined and the head is small and shapely, with neat ears and large expressive eyes. The neck is of medium length and is proudly crested in the stallions, and joins with well-sloped shoulders. The back is short and the barrel rounded and deep, while the loins are broad and strong and the croup is level, ending in a long, thick tail which is carried high.

Just as the Quarter Horse blood played an important part in the formation of a number of western breeds, so the Morgan had a vital role in the emergence of three of the best-known breeds of the eastern part of the country – the Saddlebred, the Tennessee Walking Horse and the Standardbred. The Saddlebred foundation sire was a Thoroughbred named Denmark, but it was from the Morgan that the elegant, high-stepping peacock of the show ring acquired its short coupling, rounded barrel and even temperament. The Tennessee Walking Horse, which was originally developed as an aristocratic

yet highly practical mount for the rich plantation owners and their overseers, had as its foundation sire Black Allan, a direct descendant on his dam's side of Ethan Allan, a very famous great-grandson of Justin Morgan. And among Standardbreds, the famous trotters and pacers of America's harness raceways, many are indebted to Morgan blood for a number of their sterling qualities.

The American Saddlebred is a tall horse, standing from 15·2 to 16·2hh., and is the epitome of refinement and elegance. He presents a picture of proud alertness, with extremely high carriage of head and tail. In the show ring the Saddlebred is shown in three-gaited, five-gaited, fine harness and equitation classes. The three-gaited horse performs at walk, trot and canter with much animation, and the five-gaited animal also performs the slow gait and the rack, both true four-beat gaits and spectacular to see.

The Tennessee Walking Horse is from 15·2 to 16hh., with a strong and compact build. He has a rather long head with a straight nasal profile and narrow pointed ears. The neck is fairly long and powerful, and blends with long, sloping shoulders that are one of the principal reasons for the Walking Horse's justly-famed smoothness to ride. His back is very short, his quarters are slightly sloping and his long, profuse tail is carried high and showily. The breed gives a ride completely without any jarring through the gliding flatfoot walk, the faster and spectacular running walk and the 'rocking chair' canter.

The Standardbred is as much of a racing star in the United States as is the Thoroughbred; and, interestingly enough, a grey Thoroughbred stallion named Messenger, imported into America in 1788, was the foundation sire of the breed. He sired many excellent Thoroughbreds, but it was when he was used on harness racing mares that he was found to possess exceptional prepotency that produced animals which could trot at racing speed. Standardbred harness racing horses look something like Thoroughbreds, but are heavier-boned, have flatter ribcages, longer bodies and steeper quarters. The head is not as refined as that of the Thoroughbred and is often somewhat convex, and the nostrils can flare open at an impressive degree, which is of great assistance for taking in air at speed. The breed produces both trotters and pacers.

At present America's Thoroughbreds are at the top of the international flat racing tree: in recent years racehorses bred in America have made a tremendous impact on the European racing scene and have won a disproportionate number of the most important races. Among the names of famous U.S.-bred Thoroughbreds that have raced with great success in Europe during recent years are Nijinsky, Sir Ivor, Mill Reef, Dahlia and Allez France. And their success in

Europe has meant that there has been a great upsurge in demand all over the world for American Thoroughbreds, with foreign buyers now much in evidence at the big U.S. yearling sales every year.

In America itself, one of the greatest racehorses of all time was seen in action in 1972 and 1973. This was the big chestnut Secretariat, a magnificently proportioned individual that was the first horse to win the American Triple Crown of Kentucky Derby, Preakness Stakes and Belmont Stakes in a quarter of a century.

One of the most popular breeds in the United States, and certainly one of the most versatile in the many ways that it is used by Americans, is the Arabian. Arabians are ridden in both 'English' and western styles, are used for many western competition events, star in long-distance endurance contests and are even in some States raced. In fact, admirers of the desert breed consider it to be so versatile that, in the big breed shows, many of the top saddle horses will compete with distinction both in so-called 'English' classes wearing a double bridle and an English saddle and in the Western events under cowboy tack.

However, it is in the endurance riding competitions that the Arabian really comes into his own. Pure and part bred Arabians have a spectacular record of accomplishment in America's most famous annual endurance ride, the Tevis Cup, staged in California, in which

BELOW Two Appaloosas descending. This very distinctive animal was originally bred by the Nez Percé Indians, and the skilful addition of Quarter Horse blood has developed the best specimens into eye-catching horses with lots of ability.

100 miles have to be covered in one day. The rules of the competition state that horses must be at least five years old and carry a minimum weight of 150lbs. Contestants finishing within twenty-four hours qualify for a silver and gold belt buckle, but the winner is the first horse across the finishing line, and some of them have, in fact, covered the 100 miles in less than 13 hours of riding time.

Also requiring a fair measure of endurance from horse and rider, but at a much slower pace and without the competitive element, are the long-distance trail rides, in which groups of riders, usually riding Western, ride together for several days along scenic trails, camping out under the stars at night. Naturally enough, there is great public interest in the many competitive forms of Western riding, with big crowds attending rodeos, where bronc and bull riding, steer wrestling, calf roping, cutting and reining contests are all very popular.

One distinctively American competition seen at rodeos and shows incorporating Western events is the class for Parade Horses. The cowboy saddle used is heavily decorated with silver in spectacular designs, so that the saddle is often worth more than the showy animal carrying it. American Saddlebreds of the more robust type are the first choice of many exhibitors in this contest, since the horses need to be strong indeed to perform with animation under the great weight of the silver-adorned saddles. Parade Horses must show marked animation and elevation in the parade gait, a high-stepping trot which must not be faster than five miles an hour. The class is judged 75 per cent on performance, manners and conformation, and 25 per cent on appointments.

Most Parade Horses are flashy palominos and chestnuts which have their hoofs painted gold or silver, and coloured ribbons in their long manes and tails. The riders are equally eye-catching – togged out in brightly-coloured, frilled shirts and matching trousers, often with white sombreros and ornately-tooled cowboy boots to which are attached large and much-embellished spurs.

There are a great many horse shows all over the length and breadth of the United States, with many breeds represented, and three basic distinct styles of riding – hunt seat, saddle seat and stock seat. A big four-day show will often feature many breeds and all three styles of riding, so that there is something of interest for everyone. Each day's programme will be divided into morning, afternoon and evening sessions, and some shows make sure that a bit of everything is seen each day. Yet others work out their schedules so that hunters and jumpers are featured one day, gaited breeds another and Western events on yet another day, with perhaps the final day being given over to the Championships for all the breeds and events featured during the preceding three days.

Australian Breeds and Sports

NEIL DOUGALL

The Australian horse scene is one of the most dynamic in the world today. Vigorous and expanding, as one would expect from this progressive young country, it is the home of a great variety of activities involving the horse, and has many breeds. Most of Australia's equestrian pursuits have been adapted or borrowed from other countries, principally Britain and the United States, but there are also some uniquely Australian sports and contests. The same goes for the many breeds Down Under: the bulk of them came from overseas, but the country has also produced several indigenous types in its short history.

When most people think of Australian horsemanship, their minds probably fly to mental images of the picturesque riders of the vast, lonely Outback, the tall, lean, weather-beaten stockmen with the broad-brimmed hats. Indeed these hard-riding cattlemen are the most archetypally Australian of all Down Under horsemen.

They have developed a very distinctive style of riding, based on their need to ride fast after wild cattle and half-wild horses in the rough terrain. Australia's 'ringers' (cowboys) sit deep and secure in special saddles with high pommels and cantles, long flaps, and stiff pads that jut out in front of their thighs. They ride very long, their legs almost fully extended, heels down and toes out, with the lower part of their legs so far forward that foreign horsemen claim they ride only one end of the horse.

But this question seems purely academic when the Aussie stockmen are in action at full gallop after the fleet bush cattle: then the 'ringers' and their mounts are merely swift flashes glimpsed between the trees as they gallop at breakneck speed to head off the fleeing cattle, guiding their mounts with the touch of a rein on the neck and by the split-second subtle shifting of their weight.

This typically Australian style of riding can be seen anywhere away from the coastal cities, but it is truly at home on the huge cattle stations of the Outback, where a few white men and a lot of black men have charge of some of the wildest cattle in the world.

And a renowned and highly-respected figure on the bush scene is that of the professional horsebreaker, whose skilful work often involves him in taming horses that have run free in the scrub until they are all of four or five years old!

However, don't get the idea that the work of these tough and resolute horsemen is limited to girthing a saddle on to a raging wild horse, jumping into the 'plate' and sitting tight until the animal is exhausted. While steely courage is an essential element in the taming of the powerful, half-wild horses, much knowledge and patience, and a sure and sensitive touch are needed as well.

The horses are usually driven one by one

into a round, high-fenced yard where they are lassoed, hobbled on the forefeet and 'sacked out' with a sack, a saddle blanket or an old shirt attached to the tip of a long pole. Once a horse has had enough sessions of this handling, he will allow himself to be rubbed over, and in time a saddle can be girthed on to him. Then progress is made in easy stages until a rider can climb into the saddle. However, for all the patient, skilful handling that has preceded this Moment of Truth, there is no surety that the animal will not explode into a head-plunging arc of fury when he feels a man on his back for the very first time!

Naturally enough, given the workaday base of the Outback as described above, the spectacle of rodeo is very popular in Australian country districts. Buckjumping on wild horses, bullriding atop high-humped, fierce Brahmans and bulldogging (steer wrestling) are basic to the programme, which also features American-style cutting horse contests and Australia's own campdrafting. In the latter event a stockman separates a large bullock from a group of rangy beef cattle, then drives it at the gallop around a large course marked out with upright poles, often using his bold, long-striding mount to shoulder the bullock over in the direction he wants it to go. The stockman must stay right on top of the strong, fast steer all the time in order to keep it on course, and if the beast should suddenly decide to change direction and cut under the horse's neck, both

BELOW In the all-Australian contest of campdrafting the rider guides the bullock around the course marked out with up-rights. Often he uses his mount to shoulder the big steer over in the direction in which he wants it to travel.

Stockmen at work.

BELOW Informal impromptu flat racing.

mount and man can be in for a nasty tumble on hard ground.

Another popular country sport is polo, and in certain areas, where the exciting horseback ball game has been played for generations, the standard is very high. A number of Australian polo teams have done extremely well in international tournaments from time to time, and the world-famous polo-playing Skene family, now settled in the United States, came from Australia.

Considerably more popular, though, is polocrosse – 'poor man's polo' – which is played by the ladies as well. This Aussie invention provides all the action, thrills and pleasure of polo for the enthusiastic players at only a small part of polo's cost, since in polocrosse each player needs only one mount for the entire game. The sport is rather like lacrosse on horseback: the ball is picked up in a small net at the end of a long stick, and is then carried at the gallop or thrown. The game is played in a much smaller space than is polo, so the animals do not have to gallop either as far or as hard, and therefore one pony will last an entire match.

Endurance riding contests have become popular Down Under during recent years, the main event being the Quilty Cup, which is staged during September each year over a rugged hillside course of a hundred miles in the Blue Mountains, inland from Sydney. This demanding sport, at which the Australian Stockhorse (formerly Waler) and the Arabian are stars, has been catching on fast, and a number of one-hundred-mile and fifty-mile competitive rides are held in various parts of Australia.

Racing is a major Australian sporting passion, and the most important race of the year is the almost two-mile Melbourne Cup. Australian metropolitan racecourses have really excellent

BELOW Polocrosse provides all the action, thrills and pleasure of polo for only a small part of polo's cost.

facilities for the public, since the sport is looked upon as first-class general entertainment. The big city racecourses boast spectacular lawns and flower gardens, as well as large, comfortable, modern stands. Most of the racehorses are trained at the courses, in the early morning, working on concentric training tracks inside the racecourse proper.

A very picturesque aspect of racing in Australia is provided by the 'picnic' race meetings, held in the Outback, where amateur riders and their grassfed Thoroughbreds race each other for small prizes, often only handsome trophies, on dusty, primitive bushland racecourses. Women jockeys are no novelty on this particular scene. They have been taking part in special 'ladies' bracelet' races at these meetings for many years, and in the more remote areas a good number of the 'jockeys' will be dark-skinned Aboriginal stockmen in gaudy silk shirts.

Eventing is another popular Australian equestrian sport, with the standard at the top being extremely high: the Australian Three-Day Event team won the Gold Medal at the Rome Olympics in 1960, and the Bronze Medal in Mexico City eight years later.

Trotting and pacing kindle considerable public interest, and in the big cities the trotting tracks are lavish installations where meetings are often held at night under floodlights. Trotting and pacing races are also held at agricultural shows all over the country, and the hard-fought contests around the small, circular showground tracks provide plenty of excitement.

The Australian show ring provides an abundance of other events, with show jumping a firm favourite. There is also water jumping and spectacular high jumping, a myriad of different types of classes for hacks, in-hand classes, riding contests and competitions for

FOLLOWING PAGE
ABOVE LEFT Flat racing is a major Australian sporting passion. The concentric tracks seen inside the race course proper are used for training the race horses in the early mornings.

FOLLOWING PAGE
LEFT Australian eventers are among the World's top riders: the Australian Three-Day Event team won a Gold medal at the Rome Olympics and the Bronze in Mexico City 8 years later.

BELOW
Walers. A register has been started to transform this distinctive type of horse into a breed.

harness horses and ponies.

The in-hand classes are particularly rich in variety nowadays, with classes for Thoroughbreds, Arabians, Quarter Horses, Appaloosas, American Saddlebreds, Palominos, the various breeds of British Native Ponies, Australian Ponies and Australian Stockhorses.

The latter animals are the descendants of Australia's legendary *Waler*, a horse with a soundly deserved reputation for toughness and endurance. The Waler reached the peak of its global fame during the nineteenth century and the earlier part of this century. In the days of the British presence in India the Waler was much in demand as a remount and artillery horse and during World War I more than 120,000 of these tough, dependable horses were sent to the Allied armies in Europe, the Middle East, India and Africa.

The origins of the Waler are not very clear; however, it appears that the base stock came from South Africa in the form of Cape Horses, which were the product of a mixing of Dutch, Spanish, Barb and Arabian blood. To this robust and even-tempered animal was added much blood from Britain – certainly plenty of Thoroughbred, and probably more than a touch of Cob. The resulting animal was a hardy horse standing 15 to 15·2 hh., close-coupled, with an excellent sloping shoulder, a good length of rein, a sensible head and very good limbs and feet. He had a deep chest with plenty of heart-room, and was a speedy long-strider who had developed the hard way, ranging the huge runs of the Outback.

His descendant, the Australian Stockhorse of today, has the same sterling qualities and is deservedly popular for working cattle in the bush country. An official Register has now been formed for the purpose of transforming this very definite type of horse into a distinct breed which Australia can proudly claim as her very own.

Another cattle horse that is rapidly becoming popular in Australia is the stocky, agile, fast-starting and very even-tempered Quarter Horse of the United States. The first imports of the renowned breed were made only some 20 years ago, and now there is a considerable number of quality Quarter Horses to be found

throughout the continent. Nevertheless, many
of the Aussie cowboys think that when it comes
to racing for miles after fast, wild cattle in
heavily-timbered bush country, there is nothing
to equal the long, steady, ground-consuming
stride and stamina of the Australian Stockhorse.

Stockhorses are bred on the cattle stations in
a very natural manner: the entire is loosed
to run with his band of mares in the so-called
'horse paddock' – which may well be more than
10,000 acres in area! Most often the stallion
will be a sound, well-conformed Thoroughbred
that has been retired from racing with some
distinction in one of the cities, and he will take
surprisingly little time to adapt to the life of
seeking out feed and water for himself and his

band wherever it can be found.

Another horse of the Aussie Outback is the
Brumby, the wild horse that lives in free-
ranging bands and which is determined to
remain unfettered. These untamed equines are
descendants of domesticated horses which
'went bush'; they are very tough and very,
very wily. They have the sharp-honed senses
of wild deer. Just getting close enough to
them for a good look takes a considerable
amount of bushcraft. Chasing and catching
them is something else again! Nevertheless,
there are hard-riding horsemen known as
'Brumby runners' who make a living from
capturing the wild horses by surprising them
with skilled stealth, then pursuing them across

ABOVE A picnic race meeting
at Hartz Range where
amateur riders and their grassfed Thoroughbreds compete
against each other on a dusty,
primitive bushland race
course. A good number of
the riders are always dark-
skinned aboriginal stockmen.

175

the wildest of country, frequently galloping flat out after the fleeing wild horses down steep, stony hillsides, and eventually driving them into carefully-concealed and very robust temporary stockyards.

Since racing is so popular in Australia, the breeding of Thoroughbreds is an important industry. Not only are some very high quality Thoroughbreds being produced in Australia these days, but several Australian-bred sires have done well at stud in the United States during the last few decades. Nearly all of Australia's Thoroughbreds are descended from stock imported from the British Isles, although there have been some stallion imports from France from time to time, and nowadays, with American racehorses at the top of the international tree, there have recently been some important and costly sire imports from the United States.

Australia's most famous racehorse of all time, though, was bred in neighbouring New Zealand. Popularly known as 'Big Red', he was the legendary chestnut Phar Lap, a galloper of such renown that all subsequent Australian champions have been measured against him to gauge their stature. Phar Lap won 37 of his 51 starts in just over four years of racing, and collected £66,738 in stakes, which was a very large amount indeed at the time he was racing. He died in mysterious circumstances in

America in 1932, soon after he had easily won his first and only American race.

Generally speaking, Thoroughbred brood mares are never stabled on Australian stud farms, not even for foaling. They graze outside all year round in very large paddocks, and many of them foal down unassisted in a quiet corner. Some of the most modern Thoroughbred studs in Australia have special foaling paddocks which are floodlit at night so that a close watch can be kept on any of the valuable mares which may have difficulties in foaling. Pacers and trotters are bred in the same natural way.

Highly popular today Down Under is the Arabian, which is mainly used as a pleasure mount by the 'hobby rider' in many pursuits, ranging from long-distance endurance riding to spectacularly colourful costume classes in the show ring, where riders will often tog up in authentic Bedouin costume. Most of the parent stock of Australia's Arabians came from Britain, which still sends out a lot of animals, but increasing interest is being shown in American Arabians, particularly those of Egyptian bloodlines.

British Native Ponies are also to be found in considerable numbers in Australia, with the Welsh Section A and the Shetland being the most popular in the show ring, and an increasing amount of interest being shown in the Connemara.

Considerable numbers of the American Quarter horses are now being imported to Australia and are rapidly becoming very popular.

Great Horse Competitions

ELIZABETH JOHNSON

Racing

France

Prix de l'Arc de Triomphe
First staged in 1920, the Prix de l'Arc de Triomphe has become the most prestigious event in the international racing calendar – as well as the richest. It is run annually on the first Sunday in October over a distance of $1\frac{1}{2}$ miles at the Longchamp course outside Paris.

Year	Horse	Owner	Trainer	Jockey
1960	Puissant Chef	n.a.	n.a.	M Garcia
1961	Molvedo	n.a.	n.a.	E Camici
1962	Soltikoff	n.a.	n.a.	M Delpalmas
1963	Exbury	n.a.	n.a.	J Deforge
1964	Prince Royal II	n.a.	n.a.	R Poincelet
1965	Sea Bird II	J Ternynck	E Pollet	T P Glennon
1966	Bon Mot	M F W Burmann	W Head	F Head
1967	Topyo	Mme L Volterra	C Bartholomew	W Pyers
1968	Vaguely Noble	N Bunker Hunt	M Zilber	W Williamson
1969	Levmoss	S McGrath	S McGrath	W Williamson
1970	Sassafras	M Plesch	F Mathet	Y Saint-Martin
1971	Mill Reef	P Mellon	I Balding	G Lewis
1972	San San	Comtesse Margit Batthyany	A Penna	F Head
1973	Rheingold	H R K Zeisel	B Hills	L Piggott
1974	Allez France	D Wildenstein	A Penna	Y Saint-Martin
1975	Star Appeal	W Zeitelhack	T Grieper	G Starkey
1976	Ivanjica	J Wertheimer	A Head	F Head

Prix du Jockey Club
The Prix du Jockey Club was founded in 1836 and runs annually at Chantilly over a course of $1\frac{1}{2}$ miles.

Year	Horse	Owner	Trainer	Jockey
1960	Charlottesville	HH Aga Khan	n.a.	n.a.
1961	Right Royal	Mme J Couturies	n.a.	n.a.
1962	Val de Loir	Marquise du Vivier	n.a.	n.a.
1963	Sanctus	M Ternyncks	n.a.	n.a.
1964	Le Fabuleux	Mme G Weisweiller	n.a.	n.a.
1965	Reliance	M Dupre	n.a.	n.a.
1966	Nelcius	M Duboscq	M Clement	Y Saint-Martin
1967	Astec	Baron de la Rochette	W Head	F Head
1968	Tapalque	M Plesch	F Mathet	Y Saint-Martin
1969	Goodly	M Lehmann	W Head	F Head
1970	Sassafras	M Plesch	F Mathet	Y Saint-Martin
1971	Rheffic	Mme F Dupre	F Mathet	W Pyers
1972	Hard to Beat	M Kashiyama	R Carver	L Piggott
1973	Roi Lear	Mme P Wertheimer	A Head	F Head
1974	Caracolero	Mme F Berger	F Bootin	P Paquet
1975	Val de L'Orne	M Wertheimer	A Head	F Head
1976	Youth	N Bunker Hunt	M Zilber	F Head

United Kingdom

One Thousand Guineas
Established in 1809, the One Thousand Guineas is the second of the five English Classics. It is run over a distance of one mile.

Year	Horse	Owner	Trainer	Jockey
1960	Never Too Late	Mrs H Jackson	E Pollet	R Poincelet
1961	Sweet Solera	Mrs S Castello	R Day	W Rickaby
1962	Abermaid	Mr R O'Ferrall	H Wragg	W Williamson
1963	Hula Dancer	Mrs P Widener	E Pollet	R Poincelet
1964	Pouparler	Beatrice, Lady Granard	P Prendergast	G Bougoure
1965	Night Off	Maj L Holliday	W Wharton	W Williamson
1966	Glad Rags	Mrs J Mills	M O'Brien	P Cook
1967	Fleet	Mr R Boucher	C Murless	G Moore
1968	Caergwrle	Mrs N Murless	C Murless	A Barclay
1969	Full Dress II	Mr R Moller	H Wragg	R Hutchinson
1970	Humble Duty	Jean, Lady Ashcombe	P Walwyn	L Piggott
1971	Altesse Royale	Mr F Hue-Williams	C Murless	Y Saint-Martin
1972	Waterloo	Mrs R Stanley	J Watts	E Hide
1973	Mysterious	Mr G Pope jnr	C Murless	G Lewis
1974	Highclere	HM The Queen	W Hern	J Mercer
1975	Nocturnal Spree	Mrs D O'Kelly	H Murless	J Roe
1976	Flying Water	D Wildenstein	Mr A Penna	Y Saint-Martin

Two Thousand Guineas
The Two Thousand Guineas is both the first classic race of the season and the first leg of the Triple Crown title. Held at the Newmarket Spring Meeting, it is run over a mile.

Year	Horse	Owner	Trainer	Jockey
1960	Martial	R Webster	P Prendergast	R Hutchinson
1961	Rockavon	T Yuill	G Boyd	N Stirk
1962	Privy Councillor	Maj G Glover	T Waugh	W Rickaby
1963	Only For Life	Miss M Sheriffe	J Tree	J Lindley
1964	Baldric II	Mrs H Jackson	E Fellows	W Pyers
1965	Niksar	W Harvey	W Nightingale	D Keith
1966	Kashmir II	P Butler	C Bartholomew	J Lindley
1967	Royal Palace	H Joel	N Murless	G Moore
1968	Sir Ivor	R Guest	V O'Brien	L Piggott
1969	Right Tack	J Brown	J Sutcliffe	G Lewis
1970	Nijinsky	C Engelhard	V O'Brien	L Piggott
1971	Brigadier Gerard	J Hislop	W Hern	J Mercer
1972	High Top	Sir J Thorn	B van Cutsem	W Carson
1973	Mon Fils	Mrs B Davis	R Hannon	F Durr
1974	Nonoalco	Mrs M Berger	F Boutin	Y Saint-Martin
1975	Bolkonski	C d'Alessio	H Cecil	G Dettori
1976	Wollow	C d'Alessio	H Cecil	G Dettori

The Derby

The major event of the English flat season, the Derby is held annually in June at Epsom. Instituted in 1780, reputedly after a party held to celebrate the running of the Oaks at which the Earl of Derby was present, the race is run over a distance of 1½ miles. The Derby is a supreme test of stamina and although open to both colts and fillies of three years old, it is generally run by colts. The Derby forms part of the Triple Crown, a title awarded to any horse that in one year wins the Derby, the St. Leger and the 2,000 Guineas.

Year	Horse	Owner	Trainer	Jockey
1960	St Paddy	Sir V Sassoon	N Murless	L Piggott
1961	Psidium	Mrs A Plesch	H Wragg	R Poincelet
1962	Larkspur	R Guest	V O'Brien	N Sellwood
1963	Relko	F Dupré	F Mathet	Y Saint-Martin
1964	Santa Claus	J Ismay	J Rogers	A Breasley
1965	Sea Bird II	J Ternynck	E Pollet	T Glennon
1966	Charlottown	Lady Z Wernher	G Smyth	A Breasley
1967	Royal Palace	H Joel	N Murless	G Moore
1968	Sir Ivor	R Guest	V O'Brien	L Piggott
1969	Blakeney	A Budgett	A Budgett	E Johnson
1970	Nijinsky	C Engelhard	V O'Brien	L Piggott
1971	Mill Reef	P Mellon	I Balding	G Lewis
1972	Roberto	J Galbraith	V O'Brien	L Piggott
1973	Morston	A Budgett	A Budgett	E Hide
1974	Snow Knight	Mrs N Phillips	P Nelson	B Taylor
1975	Grundy	Dr C Vittadini	P Walwyn	P Eddery
1976	Empery	N Bunker Hunt	M Zilber	L Piggott

The Oaks

Named after the 12th Earl of Derby's home and first won, in 1779, by his filly Bridget, the Oaks is the leading event of the year for three-year-old fillies and is the penultimate Classic. It is traditionally held at the same Summer Meeting at Epsom as the Derby over a distance of one mile and a half.

Year	Horse	Owner	Trainer	Jockey
1960	Never Too Late	Mrs H Jackson	E Pollet	R Poincelet
1961	Sweet Solera	Mrs S Castello	R Day	W Rickaby
1962	Monade	Mr M Goulandris	J Lieux	Y Saint-Martin
1963	Noblesse	Mrs J Olin	P Prendergast	G Bougoure
1964	Homeward Bound	Sir F Robinson	J Oxley	G Starkey
1965	Long Look	Mr J Brady	M O'Brien	J Purtell
1966	Valoris	Mr C Clore	M O'Brien	L Piggott
1967	Pia	Countess Margit Batthyany	W Elsey	E Hide
1968	La Lagune	Mr M Berlin	F Boutin	G Thiboeuf
1969	Sleeping Partner	Lord Roseberry	D Smith	J Gorton
1970	Lupe	Mrs S Joel	C Murless	A Barclay
1971	Altesse Royale	Mr F Hue-Williams	C Murless	G Lewis
1972	Ginevra	Mr C St George	H Price	A Murray
1973	Mysterious	Mr G Pope jnr	C Murless	G Lewis
1974	Polygamy	Mr L Freedman	P Walwyn	P Eddery
1975	Juliette Marney	Mr J Morrison	A Tree	L Piggott
1976	Pawneese	Mr D Wildenstein	A Penna	Y Saint-Martin

St. Leger

First run in 1776, the St. Leger is the oldest and the longest of the five British Classic races. It is held at the Doncaster course in Yorkshire and is run over a distance of 1 mile 6½ furlongs. The St. Leger takes place annually in September and forms the last leg of the Triple Crown title.

Year	Horse	Owner	Trainer	Jockey
1960	St Paddy	Sir V Sassoon	N Murless	L Piggott
1961	Aurelius	Mrs V Lilley	N Murless	L Piggott
1962	Hethersett	Maj J Holliday	W Hern	W Carr
1963	Ragusa	J Mullion	P Prendergast	G Bougoure
1964	Indiana	C Engelhard	J Watts	J Lindley
1965	Provoke	J Astor	W Hern	J Mercer
1966	Sodium	R Sigtia	G Todd	F Durr
1967	Ribocco	C Engelhard	R Houghton	L Piggott
1968	Ribero	C Engelhard	R Houghton	L Piggott
1969	Intermezzo	G Oldham	H Wragg	R Hutchinson
1970	Nijinsky	C Engelhard	V O'Brien	L Piggott
1971	Athens Wood	Mrs J Rogerson	H Thomson-Jones	L Piggott
1972	Boucher	O Phipps	V O'Brien	L Piggott
1973	Peleid	Col W Behrens	B Elsey	F Durr
1974	Bustino	Lady Beaverbrook	W Hern	J Mercer
1975	Bruni	C St George	R Price	A Murray
1976	Crow	D Wildenstein	A Penna	Y Saint-Martin

BELOW The French horse Gladiateur stunned English racegoers in 1865 by winning the Derby and St Leger.

BOTTOM Bay Middleton, one of the great English racehorses, won the Derby in 1836.

RIGHT A print of Peytona and Fashion in their great match for $20,000 over the Union course in 1845. Peytona won.

United States

Grand National
The most famous steeplechase in the world, the Grand National was first run in 1837. It is held annually in late March or early April at Aintree racecourse, Liverpool. The distance of $4\frac{1}{2}$ miles with 30 fences requires stamina and jumping ability. The course is a combination of hedges, ditches, drops and water jumps and includes the daunting Becher's Brook, a 4 ft 10 in (1.47 m) fence with a drop of over 6 ft (1.83 m), and the famous Canal Turn.

Kentucky Derby
Founded in 1875, the Kentucky Derby has become the greatest of the American classic races and forms part of the Triple Crown title awarded to any horse which wins this race together with the Preakness Stakes and the Belmont Stakes in one year. Held on the first Saturday in May over the course at Churchill Downs, Louisville, Kentucky, it is run over a distance of $1\frac{1}{4}$ miles and is open to three-year-olds.

Year	Horse	Owner	Trainer	Jockey
1960	Merryman II	Miss W Wallace	N Crump	G Scott
1961	Nicolaus Silver	C Vaughan	F Rimell	H Beasley
1962	Kilmore	N Cohen	H Price	F Winter
1963	Ayala	P Raymond	K Piggott	P Buckley
1964	Team Spirit	J Goodman	F Walwyn	G Robinson
1965	Jay Trump	Mrs N Stephenson	F Winter	Mr C Smith
1966	Anglo	S Levy	F Winter	T Norman
1967	Foinavon	C Watkins	J Kempton	J Buckingham
1968	Red Alligator	J Manners	D Smith	B Fletcher
1969	Highland Wedding	T McKoy	G Balding	E Harty
1970	Gay Trip	A Chambers	F Rimell	P Taaffe
1971	Specify	F Pontin	J Sutcliffe	J Cooke
1972	Well To Do	Capt T Forster	T Forster	G Thorner
1973	Red Rum	N le Mare	D McCain	B Fletcher
1974	Red Rum	N le Mare	D McCain	B Fletcher
1975	L'Escargot	R Guest	D Moore	T Carberry
1976	Rag Trade	P Raymond	F Rimell	J Burke

Year	Horse	Owner	Trainer	Jockey
1960	Venetian Way	Sunny Blue Farm	V Sovinski	W Hartack
1961	Carry Back	Mrs K Price	J Price	J Sellers
1962	Decidedly	El Peco Ranch	H Luro	W Hartack
1963	Chateaugay	Darby Dan Farm	J Conway	B Baeza
1964	Northern Dancer	Winfields Farm	H Luro	W Hartack
1965	Lucky Debonair	Mrs A Rice	F Catrone	W Shoemaker
1966	Kauai King	Ford Stable	H Forrest	D Brumfield
1967	Proud Clarion	Darby Dan Farm	L Gentry	R Ussery
1968	Dancer's Image	P Fuller	L Cavalaris	R Ussery
1969	Majestic Prince	F McMahon	J Longden	W Hartack
1970	Dust Commander	R Lehmann	D Combs	M Manganello
1971	Canonero II	E Caibett	J Arias	G Avita
1972	Riva Ridge	Meadow Stable	L Lauren	R Turcotte
1973	Secretariat	Meadow Stable	L Lauren	R Turcotte
1974	Cannonade	J Olin	W Stephens	A Cordero
1975	Foolish Pleasure	J L Greer	L Jolley	J Vasquez
1976	Bold Forbes	E R Tizol	L S Barrera	A Cordero

Preakness Stakes

The Preakness Stakes were first held in 1873 and now take place annually in the middle of May. The race, held over a distance of 9½ furlongs at the Pimlico course, Maryland, constitutes one third of the Triple Crown.

Year	Horse	Owner	Trainer	Jockey
1960	Bally Ache	Turfland	H Pitt	R Ussery
1961	Carry Back	Mrs K Price	J Price	J Sellers
1962	Greek Money	Brandywine Stable	V Raines	J Rotz
1963	Candy Spots	R Ellsworth	M Tenney	W Shoemaker
1964	Northern Dancer	Winfields Farm	H Luro	W Hartack
1965	Tom Rolfe	Powhatan	F Whiteley jnr	R Turcotte
1966	Kauai King	M Ford	H Forrest	D Brumfield
1967	Damascus	E Bancroft	F Whiteley jnr	W Shoemaker
1968	Forward Pass	Calumet Farm	H Forrest	I Valenzuela
1969	Majestic Prince	F McMahon	J Longden	W Hartack
1970	Personality	E Jacobs	J Jacobs	E Belmonte
1971	Canonero II	E Caibett	J Arias	G Avila
1972	Bee Bee Bee	W Farish 3rd	D Carroll	E Nelson
1973	Secretariat	Meadow Stable	L Lauren	R Turcotte
1974	Little Current	Darby Dan Farm	L Rondinello	M Rivera
1975	Master Derby	Golden Chance Farms Inc	W E Adams	D G McHargue
1976	Elocutionist	E C Cashmam	P T Adwell	J Lively

Belmont Stakes

First held in 1867, the Belmont Stakes are regarded by some as the most important of the Triple Crown races. The race is run over a distance of 1½ miles at its now permanent home at Belmont Park, New York.

Year	Horse	Owner	Trainer	Jockey
1960	Celtic Ash	J O'Connell	T Barry	W Hartack
1961	Sherluck	J Sher	H Young	B Baeza
1962	Jaipur	G Widener	B Mulholland	W Shoemaker
1963	Chateaugay	J Galbreath	J Conway	B Baeza
1964	Quadrangle	P Mellon	J. Burch	M Ycaza
1965	Hail to All	Mrs B Cohen	E Yowell	J Sellers
1966	Amberoid	R Webster	L Lauren	W Boland
1967	Damascus	Mrs E Bancroft	F Whiteley jnr	W Shoemaker
1968	Stage Door Johnny	Greentree Stable	J Gaver	H Gustines
1969	Arts and Letters	P Mellon	E Burch	B Baeza
1970	High Echelon	Mrs E Jacobs	J Jacobs	J Rotz
1971	Pass Catcher	October House Farm	E Yowell	W Blum
1972	Riva Ridge	Meadow Stable	L Lauren	R Turcotte
1973	Secretariat	Meadow Stable	L Lauren	R Turcotte
1974	Little Current	Darby Dan Farm	L Rondinello	M Rivera
1975	Avatar	A A Seeligson jnr	A T Doyle	W Shoemaker
1976	Tell Me All	Hobeau Farm	H Jerkens	J Ruane

Heading for the final stretch.

South Africa

Durban July Handicap

The most important and richest race in South Africa, the Durban July Handicap is run over 10½ furlongs at Turffentein outside Johannesburg.

Year	Horse	Owner	Trainer	Jockey
1960	Left Wing	Birch Bros	n.a.	n.a.
1961	Kerason	Gp Capt Dalzell	n.a.	n.a.
1962	Diza	F Lambert	J H Gorton	A Roberts
1963	Colorado King	P S Louw	S Laird	n.a.
1964	Numeral	C W Engelhard	n.a.	n.a.
1965	King Willow	Mr & Mrs H Oppenheimer	J Breval	I Bailey
1966	Java Head	B Levin	S Laird	H Cawcutt
1967	Sea Cottage	S Laird	S Laird	R Sivewright
1968	Chimboraa	Mr & Mrs Burstein	B A Cherry	D Payne
1969	Naval Escort	D & C V Saunders	A Reid	F W Rickaby
1970	Court Day	M Livanos	R T Knight	n.a.
1971	Mazarin	Mr & Mrs T Tenderini	S C Laird	R Sivewright
1972	In Full Flight	N Ferguson	n.a.	n.a.
1973	Yataghan	J M Scrimmel	S C Laird	Bertie Hayden
1974	Ribovilla	Mr & Mrs G Mosenthal	G Azzie	M Schoeman
1975	Principal Boy*	n.a.	n.a.	n.a.
1976	Jamaican Music	Dr C A Crobin	Ralph Rixon	Bertie Abercrombie

*Gatecrasher came in first but was disqualified and put back to third place.

Three-day Event

Three-day eventing, also known as horse-trialing and combined training, dates from the days of the great military academies. The idea originated as a means of testing an officer and his charger in every aspect of equitation; indeed, it is still often referred to as the 'militaire'.

This event is an arduous competition for horse and rider which is completed over three consecutive days. It demonstrates all the skills of the rider and his mount in every discipline of the art. The first day consists of a demonstration of obedience in the form of an advanced dressage test, followed on the second day by a test of speed and endurance over road-and-tracks, steeplechasing and cross-country. The final day is devoted to show jumping. The scores are tallied in penalties and the horse and rider with the lowest score for the three days is the winner.

World Three-day Event Championships

Year	Team	Individual	Horse	Country
1966	1 Ireland	1 Capt C Moratorio	Chalan	Argentina
	2 Argentina	2 R Meade	Barberry	Gt Britain
	All other teams eliminated	3 V Freeman-Mason	Sam Weller	Ireland
1970	1 Gt Britain	1 M Gordon-Watson	Cornishman V	Gt Britain
	2 France	2 R Meade	The Poacher	Gt Britain
	All other teams eliminated	3 J Wofford	Kilkenny	USA
1974	1 USA	1 B Davidson	Irish Cap	USA
	2 Gt Britain	2 M Plumb	Good Mixture	USA
	3 W Germany	3 H Thomas	Playamar	Gt Britain

European Three-day Event Championships

Year	Team	Individual	Horse	Country
1962	1 USSR	1 Capt J Templer	M'Lord Connolly	Gt Britain
	2 Ireland	2 G Gasumov	Granj	USSR
	3 Gt Britain	3 J Wykeham-Musgrave	Ryebrooks	Gt Britain
1965	1 USSR	1 M Babierecki	Volt	Poland
	2 Ireland	2 L Baklyshkin	Ruon	USSR
	3 Gt Britain	3 H Karsten	Condora	W Germany
1967	1 Gt Britain	1 Maj E Boylan	Durlas Eile	Ireland
	2 Ireland	2 M Whiteley	The Poacher	Gt Britain
	3 France	3 Maj D Allhusen	Lochinvar	Gt Britain
1969	1 Gt Britain	1 M Gordon-Watson	Cornishman V	Gt Britain
	2 USSR	2 R Walker	Pasha	Gt Britain
	3 W Germany	3 B Messman	Windspiel	W Germany
1971	1 Gt Britain	1 HRH Princess Anne	Doublet	Gt Britain
	2 USSR	2 D West	Baccarat	Gt Britain
	3 Ireland	3 S Stevens	Classic Chips	Gt Britain
1973	1 W Germany	1 A Evdokimov	Jeger	USSR
	2 USSR	2 H Blöcker	Albrandt	W Germany
	3 Gt Britain	3 H Karsten	Sioux	W Germany
1975	1 USSR	1 L Prior-Palmer	Be Fair	Gt Britain
	2 Gt Britain	2 HRH Princess Anne	Goodwill	Gt Britain
	3 W Germany	3 P Gornuschko	Gusar	USSR

Badminton Horse Trials

The Badminton Horse Trials is a three-day eventing competition which takes place annually in April, weather permitting. They were first held in 1949 at the invitation of the Duke of Beaufort in the grounds of his estate at Badminton House, Gloucestershire, from where the name originated. In common with other three-day events, the first day is devoted to dressage, the second to tests of speed and endurance and the third to show jumping. The Badminton Horse Trials is a severe test to both horse and rider and since its inception has become a classic international event.

Year	Rider	Horse	Country
1960	W Roycroft	Our Solo	Australia
1961	L Morgan	Salad Days	Australia
1962	Miss A Drummond-Hay	Merely-A-Monarch	Gt Britain
1963	(cancelled owing to bad weather)		
1964	Capt J R Templer	M'Lord Connolly	Gt Britain
1965	Maj E A Boylan	Durlas Eile	Ireland
1966	(cancelled owing to bad weather)		
1967	Miss C Ross-Taylor	Jonathan	Gt Britain
1968	Miss J Bullen	Our Nobby	Gt Britain
1969	R Walker	Pasha	Gt Britain
1970	R Meade	The Poacher	Gt Britain
1971	Lt M Phillips	Great Ovation	Gt Britain
1972	Lt M Phillips	Great Ovation	Gt Britain
1973	Miss L Prior-Palmer	Be Fair	Gt Britain
1974	Capt M Phillips	Colombus	Gt Britain
1975	cancelled		
1976	Janet Hodgson	Larkspur	Gt Britain

Show Jumping

Regarded by many as a 'Circus art' during the early years of this century, show jumping really only became accepted as an equestrian sport after 1945, and with the help of television and the media, is now one of the most popular spectator sports in any sphere.

Courses, fences and competitors have far advanced. Many international events offer high prize money and with the introduction of sponsorship can be highly lucrative for owners and riders.

Each horse must be registered with its national show jumping association and all are graded as to their ability and prize winnings. The judging of competitions is by calculating faults incurred at each fence, there are no penalties for style, or lack of it.

Show jumping is today governed by the Fédération Equestre Internationale and it is they who draw up and amend the rules. Should a fence be knocked down or lowered in height, four faults are incurred; refusals warrant three faults on the first occasion, six on the second, and elimination on the third. A fall of horse and rider incurs eight faults. There are no penalties for rapping or knocking the obstacle. Each course has to be completed within a time limit, calculated on 300 yards per minute; competitors exceeding the limit are penalized at the rate of $\frac{1}{4}$ fault per second.

The winner is the competitor who completes the course with the least number of faults or, in the event of a tie, after a timed jump-off.

President's Cup

An international show jumping championship instituted in 1965. A trophy is awarded annually to the national team gaining the most points in Prix des Nations events (Nation's Cups) between December 1st and November 30th over a twelve-month period. Nation's Cups are held only at official international horse shows.

Year	Country	Year	Country
1965	1 Gt Britain	1971	1 W Germany
	2 W Germany		2 Gt Britain
	3 Italy		3 Italy
1966	1 USA	1972	1 Gt Britain
	2 Spain		2 W Germany
	3 France		3 Italy
1967	1 Gt Britain	1973	1 Gt Britain
	2 W Germany		2 W Germany
	3 Italy		3 Switzerland
1968	1 USA	1974	1 Gt Britain
	2 Gt Britain		2 W Germany
	3 { Italy		3 France
	{ W Germany	1975	1 W Germany
1969	1 W Germany		2 Gt Britain
	2 Gt Britain		3 { Italy
	3 Italy		{ Belgium
1970	1 Gt Britain	1976	1 W. Germany
	2 W Germany		2 France
	3 Italy		3 { Ireland
			{ Italy

Men's European Championship

Year	Rider	Horse	Country
1961	1 D Broome	Sunsalve	Gt Britain
	2 Capt P d'Inzeo	Pioneer	Italy
	3 H Winkler	Romanus	W Germany
1962	1 C Barker	Mister Softee	Gt Britain
	2 { H Winkler	Romanus	W Germany
	{ Capt P d'Inzeo	The Rock	Italy
1963	1 G Mancinelli	Rockette	Italy
	2 A Schockemöhle	Freiherr	W Germany
	3 H Smith	O'Malley	Gt Britain
1964	No competition		
1965	1 H Schridde	Dozent II	W Germany
	2 A Queipo de Llano	Infernal	Spain
	3 A Schockemöhle	Exakt	W Germany
1966	1 N Pessoa	Gran Geste	Brazil
	2 F Chapot	San Lucas	USA
	3 H Arrambide	Chimbote	Argentina
1967	1 D Broome	Mister Softee	Gt Britain
	2 H Smith	Harvester	Gt Britain
	3 A Schockemöhle	Donald Rex	W Germany
1968	No competition		
1969	1 D Broome	Mister Softee	Gt Britain
	2 A Schockemöhle	Donald Rex	W Germany
	3 H Winkler	Enigk	W Germany
1971	1 H Steenken	Simona	W Germany
	2 H Smith	Evan Jones	Gt Britain
	3 P Weier	Wulf	Switzerland
1972	No competition		
1973	1 P McMahon	Pennwood Forge Mill	Gt Britain
	2 A Schockemöhle	The Robber	W Germany
	3 H Parot	Tic	France
1974	No competition		
1975	1 A. Schockemöhle	Warwick	W Germany
	2 H Steenken	Erle	W Germany
	3 S Sonksen	Kwept	W Germany
1976	No competition		

Men's World Championship

Year	Rider	Horse	Country
1960	1 Capt R d'Inzeo	Gowran Girl	Italy
	2 C Delia	Duipil	Argentina
	3 D Broome	Sunsalve	Gt Britain
1966	1 P d'Oriola	Pomone B	France
	2 A de Bohorques	Quizas	Spain
	3 Capt R d'Inzeo	Bowjak	Italy
1970	1 D Broome	Beethoven	Gt Britain
	2 G Mancinelli	Fidux	Italy
	3 H Smith	Mattie Brown	Gt Britain
1974	1 H Steenken	Simona	W Germany
	2 E Macken	Pele	Ireland
	3 { F Chapot	Main Spring	USA
	{ H Simon	Lavendel	Austria

Women's World Championship

Year	Rider	Horse	Country
1965	1 Miss M Coakes	Stroller	Gt Britain
	2 Miss K Kusner	Untouchable	USA
	3 Miss A Westwood	The Maverick	Gt Britain
1970	1 Miss J Lefebvre	Rocket	France
	2 Mrs M Mould	Stroller	Gt Britain
	3 Miss A Drummond-Hay	Merely-A-Monarch	Gt Britain
1974	1 Mrs J Tissot	Rocket	France
	2 Miss M McEvoy	Mr Muskie	USA
	3 Miss B Kerr	Magnor	Canada

Women's European Championship

Year	Rider	Horse	Country
1960	1 Miss S Cohen	Clare Castle	Gt Britain
	2 Mrs W Wofford	Hollandia	Gt Britain
	3 Miss A Clement	Nico	W Germany
1961	1 Miss P Smythe	Flanagan	Gt Britain
	2 Miss I Jansen	Icare	Holland
	3 Miss C Cancre	Ocean	France
1962	1 Miss P Smythe	Flanagan	Gt Britain
	2 Mrs H Kohler	Cremona	W Germany
	3 Mrs P de Goyoaga	Kif Kif	Spain
1963	1 Miss P Smythe	Flanagan	Gt Britain
	2 Mrs A Givaudan	Huipil	Brazil
	3 Miss A Drummond-Hay	Merely-A-Monarch	Gt Britain
1966	1 Miss J Lefebvre	Kenavo	France
	2 Miss M Bachmann	Sandro	Switzerland
	3 Miss L Novo	Oxo Bob	Italy
1967	1 Miss K Kusner	Untouchable	USA
	2 Miss L Novo	Predestine	Italy
	3 Miss M Bachmann	Erbach	Switzerland
1968	1 Miss A Drummond-Hay	Merely-A-Monarch	Gt Britain
	2 Miss G Serventi	Gay Monarch	Italy
	3 { Miss M Coakes	Stroller	Gt Britain
	{ Miss J Lefebvre	Rocket	France
1969	1 Miss I Kellet	Morning Light	Ireland
	2 Miss A Drummond-Hay	Xanthos	Gt Britain
	3 Miss A Westwood	The Maverick	Gt Britain
1971	1 Miss A Moore	Psalm	Gt Britain
	2 Mrs M Dawes	The Maverick	Gt Britain
	3 Miss M Leiten-Berger	Limbarra de Porto Conte	Austria
1973	1 Miss A Moore	Psalm	Gt Britain
	2 Miss C Bradley	True Lass	Gt Britain
	3 Mrs P Weier	Erbach	Switzerland
1974	No competition		
1975	Combined with Men's European Championship		
1976	No competition		

Olympic Games

Equestrian events were first included in the 1912 Olympic Games held at Stockholm, mostly due to the efforts of Count Clarence von Rosen, Master of the Horse to the King of Sweden. There are now three disciplines for competition: dressage, three-day event and show jumping. In dressage, the team and individual competitions are judged as two separate events, with the top 12 competitors from the team section going forward to the individual ride-off. The three-day event has three phases: dressage test, cross country and show jumping. In the cross country, the team and individual winners are decided simultaneously to avoid over-exerting the horses. In the show jumping, an individual event is now held separately preceding the Prix des Nations, which is traditionally held as the final event of the Olympic Games. Countries may nominate different horses and riders for each event, that is three to jump individually and then, if necessary, another four to take part in the team competition. Of the four members of the team competition, the score of the best three competitors is to count over two rounds. No prize money is given and there are no individual awards.

Dressage

Year	Team	Individual	Horse	Country
1960	No team awards	1 S Filatov	Absent	USSR
		2 G Fischer	Wald	Switzerland
		3 J Neckermann	Asbach	Germany*
1964	1 Germany*	1 H Chammartin	Woermann	Switzerland
	2 Switzerland	2 H Boldt	Remus	Germany*
	3 USSR	3 S Filatov	Absent	USSR
1968	1 W Germany	1 I Kisimov	Ikhov	USSR
	2 USSR	2 J Neckermann	Mariano	W Germany
	3 Switzerland	3 R Klimke	Dux	W Germany
1972	1 USSR	1 L Linsenhoff	Piaff	W Germany
	2 W Germany	2 E Petushkova	Pepel	USSR
	3 Sweden	3 J Neckermann	Venetia	W Germany
1976	1 W Germany	1 C Stuckelberger	Granat	Switzerland
	2 Switzerland	2 H Boldt	Woycek	W Germany
	3 USA	3 Dr R Klimke	Mehmed	W Germany

Three-day Event

Year	Team	Individual	Horse	Country
1960	1 Australia	1 L Morgan	Salad Days	Australia
	2 Switzerland	2 N Lavis	Mirrabooka	Australia
	3 France	3 A Buhler	Gay Spark	Switzerland
1964	1 Italy	1 M Checcoli	Surbean	Italy
	2 USA	2 C Moratorio	Chalan	Argentina
	3 Germany*	3 F Ligges	Don Kosak	Germany*
1968	1 Gt Britain	1 J-J Guyon	Pitou	France
	2 USA	2 Maj D Allhusen	Lochinvar	Gt Britain
	3 Australia	3 M Page	Foster	USA
1972	1 Gt Britain	1 R Meade	Laurieston	Gt Britain
	2 USA	2 A Argenton	Woodland	Italy
	3 W Germany	3 J Jonsson	Sarajevo	Sweden
1976	1 USA	1 T Coffin	Bally Cor	USA
	2 W Germany	2 M Plumb	Better and Better	USA
	3 Australia	3 K Schultz	Madrigal	W Germany

Show Jumping

Year	Team	Individual	Horse	Country
1960	1 Germany*	1 Capt R d'Inzeo	Possillipo	Italy
	2 USA	2 Capt P d'Inzeo	The Rock	Italy
	3 Italy	3 D Broome	Sunsalve	Gt Britain
1964	1 Germany*	1 P d'Oriola	Lutteur	France
	2 France	2 H Shridde	Dozent	Germany*
	3 Italy	3 P Robeson	Firecrest	Gt Britain
1968	1 Canada	1 W Steinkraus	Snowbound	USA
	2 France	2 Miss M Coakes	Stroller	Gt Britain
	3 W Germany	3 D Broome	Mister Softee	Gt Britain
1972	1 W Germany	1 G Mancinelli	Ambassador	Italy
	2 USA	2 Miss A Moore	Psalm	Gt Britain
	3 Italy	3 N Shapiro	Sloopy	USA
1976	1 France	1 A Schockemöhle	Warwick Rex	W Germany
	2 W Germany	2 M Vaillancourt	Branch County	Canada
	3 Belgium	3 F Mathy	Gai Luron	Belgium

*Prior to 1968 West and East Germany sent a joint team to the Olympic Games

183

Glossary

ELIZABETH JOHNSON

Above the bit An evasion of the bit, when the horse raises its head to avoid the action of the bit in its mouth, thereby reducing any effective control the rider has over the horse. This habit is remedied by constant schooling to lower the head and have the horse accept the bit.

Action The manner in which a horse moves. Good action is when he plants all four feet freely and with equal weight on each foot at every pace. Bad action is when a horse moves unevenly or with an unlevel gait; 'tied in' action is when a horse cannot extend its limbs to move freely.

Aged A term used for any horse or pony over eight years. Age up to eight years can be judged accurately by inspecting the teeth, after this age it becomes increasingly difficult to judge with certainty.

Aids The signals, through hands, legs, seat and voice whereby the rider communicates his wishes to the horse. Artificial aids are whip, spurs, and various items of equipment that form part of the saddlery, such as martingales.

Airs above the ground A form of *haute école* where the horse is elevated off the ground in some form of leap or jump. This is performed only by the most advanced horses, such as the stallions of the Spanish Riding School.

Albino A colour-type of horse rather than a breed. The true albino has white hair, pink skin and blue-tinted eyes, as it lacks any true pigmentation. The Albino Horse is recognized in America as a colour type.

Azoturia Often known as Monday Morning Disease, because it affects horses that have been left standing in on a Sunday. It is a blood disorder that causes the muscles to atrophy and seize up if too much heating food is given without enough exercise.

Bag fox A fox that is caught and kept and then released for the purpose of hunting. This practice is not approved by the hunting fraternity.

Bandages A form of support and protection against cold and injury. They are used on a working horse, usually on the legs but also to protect the tail while travelling or to keep it in a tidy state while the horse is in the stable.

Bang Method of cutting the tail squarely with scissors.

Bars There are various different 'bars' related to the horse and its equipment: the bars of the mouth, are the sensitive areas of the horse's lips where the bit lies; the bars of the foot divide the sole from the frog; the bars of a saddle are the metal parts to which the stirrups are attached; the bars of the bit are the cheek pieces on any form of curb bit.

Bay The reddish-brown colour of a horse which also possesses black mane and tail and black points on the limbs.

Bedding The form of bedding that is used in a stable can vary from straw to wood chips, to sawdust or even peat. This provides a soft surface upon which the horse can lie in the stable without injury to itself. Bedding must be changed regularly to ensure a healthy horse.

Bit The metal part of the bridle that is placed in the horse's mouth. There are many variations, but the two main types are the snaffle and the curb bit.

Blacksmith The man who makes horseshoes and then fits them to each foot of the horse. This is a skilled craft and one that seemed, for some time to be dying out. Farriery, as the craft is called, is now on the increase and apprentice-training schemes are in operation.

Blaze A white mark running down the centre of a horse's face.

Blister A form of medication; by rubbing an irritant on to an affected area, the blood supply to the injured area is increased, thereby hastening recovery.

Body brush A soft bristled brush essential for the grooming of a horse, as it removes the dirt and sweat from the body. It is normally used in conjunction with a curry comb, and the comb is used at regular intervals to clean the brush.

Bolt A dangerous vice in any horse causing it to gallop in an uncontrolled manner with little regard either for its own safety or for that of its rider. This is highly dangerous, especially in a child's pony.

Boot jack A wooden device to aid in the removal of hunting boots by fitting the heel into a shaped piece of wood and then pulling.

Bran The husk of the wheat grain that is separated after milling. This bulk food is an essential part of a horse's diet, especially if the horse is off work for any period of time. It acts as a laxative when given as a hot mash with Epsom salts.

Breaking in A term used to describe the early education of a young horse from the time it is first subjected to human influence until it has become a mannered and rideable animal.

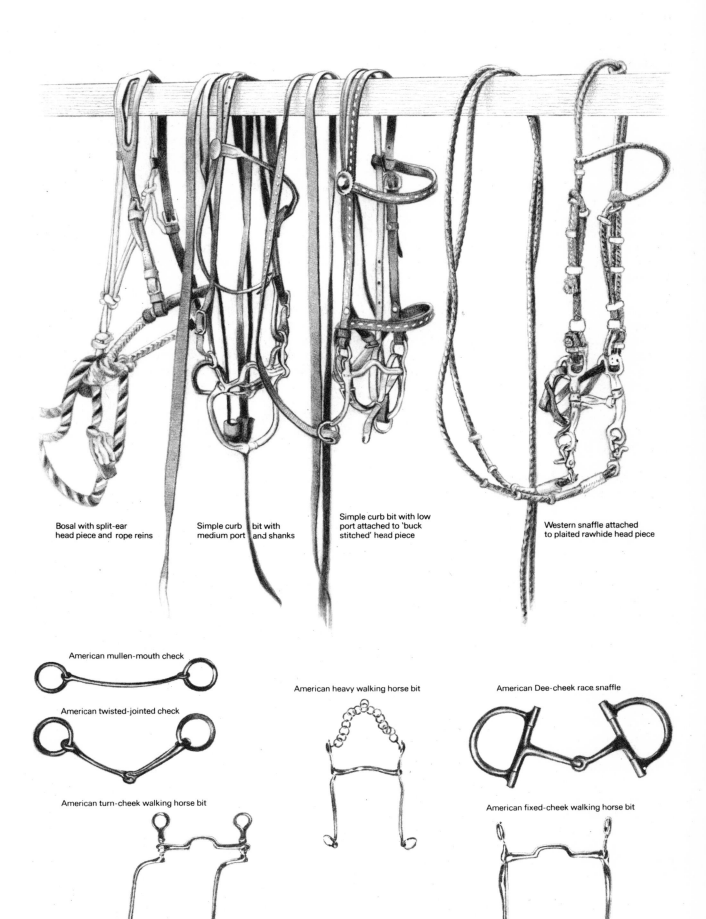

Bosal with split-ear
head piece and rope reins

Simple curb bit with
medium port and shanks

Simple curb bit with low
port attached to 'buck
stitched' head piece

Western snaffle attached
to plaited rawhide head piece

American mullen-mouth check

American twisted-jointed check

American heavy walking horse bit

American Dee-cheek race snaffle

American turn-cheek walking horse bit

American fixed-cheek walking horse bit

185

Bridle The equipment that fits over the horse's head, with a bit in the mouth to enable the rider to control the movement of the horse and guide the direction of movement. Bridles take many forms, the simplest being a snaffle bit with a plain noseband, one pair of reins, a throat lash headpiece, cheek pieces and a browband. This equipment is normally made of leather.

Bridlepath A path over which there is a right-of-way for horses as opposed to a footpath which is restricted to walkers on foot.

Broken-kneed A horse with blemishes on both knees showing that it has at some stage in its past been 'down' on its knees. A definite disadvantage in selling a horse.

Broken-winded A horse is said to be broken-winded when the air sacs in the lungs have been ruptured for any one of a variety of reasons, one being over-exertion of an unfit horse. Often the horse will have a chronic cough and will clearly be unable to perform any really hard and fast work.

Brood mare A mare used solely for breeding purposes.

Brush 'Brushing' is a faulty action in a horse where the inside of one foot knocks into the lower part of the other leg and causes injury. 'Brushing boots' can be used to prevent injury.

Brush fence A fence built to simulate a hedge.

Buck The action of a horse whereby he lowers his head, raises his hind legs in a kick, and attempts to dislodge his rider if he has one.

Calkin A projecting piece of metal positioned at the end (heel) of a horseshoe to give extra grip, rather like a stud that can be inserted into a specially prepared hole in the shoe.

Cannon bone The lower bone in the horse's front leg, the equivalent of the shin bone in the human.

Canter A three-time pace that preceeds the gallop of racing pace. There are several forms of canter: collected, ordinary, extended, counter, disunited.

Caprilli Federico Caprilli was the Italian inventor of the forward seat in riding.

Cavaletti A series of low, wooden jumps that can be easily moved for schooling purposes and altered in height and width by building them in different combinations. Invaluable for schooling horses.

Chaff An important part of a stabled horse's diet, chaff is the result of chopping hay into small pieces. It acts as a bulk feed in the daily diet.

Chestnut Colour of horses, usually a bright red-brown, but it can vary from a very yellowy brown to a really deep reddish-brown. Mane and tail are usually of the same colour although some horses may have flaxen-coloured manes and tails.

Clip The process of removing the horse's winter coat with electric clippers to enable it to work through the winter without sweating unduly and so lose condition or catch a chill. Once clipped, horses have to be kept in stables and clothed adequately to compensate for the loss of the winter coat.

Cob A horse between 14hh. and 15hh., strongly built with short, tough limbs.

Colic The name given to acute stomach-ache in the horse, it is highly dangerous if not treated immediately, as the horse can injure itself during the spasms of acute pain. Drenches can be given, and the horse should be kept walking to prevent it lying down and if necessary, veterinary advice should be sought.

Colt A young male horse, uncastrated or ungelded.

Corns Inflamed areas in the foot, often caused by bad shoeing or neglect of shoes. They result in pain and lameness.

Couple Hounds are always referred to in couples, i.e., $3\frac{1}{2}$ couples equals 7 hounds; $\frac{1}{2}$ a couple is one hound.

Crib-biting A vice which is often developed through boredom, when the horse grabs with its teeth any available fixed object, i.e. the manger or crib and sucks wind through its open mouth. This can cause harm to the wind and digestion and is therefore extremely undesirable.

Dandy brush A stiff bristled brush used for removing mud and dried sweat from the coat.

Dishing An exaggerated movement of the front legs where the feet describe an outward movement as well as the normal forward action.

Dock The root of the tail.

Double bridle A bridle with two bits, a snaffle and a curb bit, normally used for showing horses and in advanced dressage as it demands a greater degree of collection and flexion than an ordinary snaffle bridle.

Dressage The art of schooling a horse to produce the required movements at a certain time and place within an enclosed arena. The dressage test is the first part of a three day event, to prove that the horse has been correctly educated and schooled to a reasonable level. The more advanced dressage movements may take years to perfect.

Dun The yellowish colour often found in the Connemara breed. Frequently there is a dorsal stripe in black, but a true Dun must have black skin under the hair and a black mane and tail. A blue dun is, as its name suggests, a variation with a grey/blue coat colour.

Ergot The horny growth often apparent in ponies at the back of the fetlock joint.

Extensions The exaggeration of the normal paces, i.e., an extended trot is an extended version of the trot pace, when the horse deliberately points its toes and really stretches its limbs.

BELOW LEFT Half pass.
BELOW RIGHT Full pass.

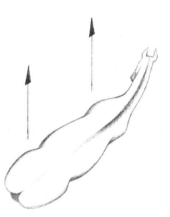

FEI Fédération Equestre International – the international governing body of all matters equestrian, excluding racing, based in Brussels. HRH Prince Philip is President of the FEI.

Feed General term given to all horse fodder.

Field The term used to describe the mounted followers of a hunt excluding the hunt servants and the Master.

Filly A young female horse.

Firing A process of applying hot irons to the horse's legs to help repair broken-down tendons. The act of firing sets up scar tissue that acts as a permanent bandage. Many racehorses are fired and continue to work adequately.

Forelock The lock of hair that falls between the ears. It is an extension of the mane.

Frog The part of the horse's foot that acts as the concussion pad during work.

Fullering To put a groove into the horse shoe to aid its grip on slippery roads. Most hunter shoes are fullered.

Full pass An advanced dressage movement in which the horse moves laterally without gaining any forward ground.

Gag bit An extremely severe form of bit used on horses that pull hard.

Gall A sore produced by harness rubbing on parts of the body, most common around the girth or under the saddle in riding horses.

Gallop The fastest pace of a horse.

Gamgee A form of cotton wool for use under exercise or travelling bandages.

Gelding A castrated male horse.

Girth The strap under the horse's stomach that holds the saddle in place. There are a variety of types, made of leather, nylon, string and webbing.

Go spare When a horse gets away from its rider and runs loose.

Groom The act of brushing the horse in order to keep it clean and in healthy condition. This is a vital everyday task.

Gymkhana Various games on horseback are known as gymkhana games, mainly held for ponies and children.

Hack A riding horse. The term is now mainly used to describe a show horse. To go for a hack means to go for a ride.

Hackney A specialized breed of driving horse or pony characterised by the exaggerated action at the trot.

Half-pass A lateral movement used in schooling the horse to a fairly high standard, where the horse moves both sideways and forwards.

Halter or headcollar Made of either leather or rope, this is the piece of harness used for leading horses to and from fields and stables, and for tying up etc. It has no bit, and is usually used in conjunction with a headcollar rope or chain.

Hand The accepted measurement for horses, a hand measuring 10cm (4in). A horse is said to be 15.2hh., meaning 15 hands two inches and is measured to its withers from the ground.

Hay Dried grass gathered in early summer and baled and stored for winter feed. It is an essential part of a horse's diet if stabled.

Hay net A string or rope net which contains the hay and prevents wastage.

High School Extremely advanced dressage, *haute école*, of the type practised by the Spanish Riding School.

Hindquarters The rear end of the horse including the back legs.

Hobday A form of operation on the horse's larynx to assist breathing.

Hock The large joint on the back leg between the second thigh and the hind cannon, which corresponds to the human heel.

Hogged mane A mane cut short, level with the neck, popular for cobby types.

Hoof The foot of the horse.

Hoof pick Curved metal instrument for cleaning out the feet.

Hunter A type of horse rather than a breed, suited for hunting over varied terrain and capable of jumping, and galloping for long distances. Hunter classes take up a large portion of the major horse shows and champion horses in these classes frequently fetch large prices when sold.

In hand A horse which is led from the ground.

Irish martingale Two rings joined by a short leather strap that slip over the reins to prevent the horse from confusing the reins if he tends to throw his head.

Irons The stirrup irons, part of the saddlery for a riding horse.

Jibbing Refusal of a horse to pass a certain point or object. Horse remains rooted to the spot or runs backwards.

Jogging An annoying habit often found in excitable horses that refuse to walk or trot properly but insist on jogging, a most uncomfortable pace.

Jumping lane An enclosed lane for loose schooling a horse over jumps without the rider.

Jute rugs Most stable rugs are made of jute (a form of sacking), lined with wool.

Kaolin poultice A fine clay-type poultice that is invaluable in reducing inflammation and swelling on horses' legs when applied hot.

Kicking A dangerous vice, especially when aimed at humans or other horses and most dangerous when out hunting or with a gathering of other horses.

Knee caps Protective covering made of leather and rugging for the knees, used when travelling or occasionally when working on slippery road surfaces.

Laminitis Fever in the horse's feet, caused by too much rich grass, especially common in ponies in the spring.

Lash The small piece of silk attached to the end of the thong on a hunting whip which makes the cracking sound.

Leathers The stirrup straps.

Linseed A seed that has to be thoroughly cooked before feeding to horses, but which is very beneficial in putting on flesh and a lovely bloom to the coat. Can be fed as a mash or as gruel after a hard day's work.

Litter Another term for the bedding used in stables.

Livery A horse at livery is one which is boarded at a stable away from the owner's home; a livery fee will be charged.

Loose box A stable where a horse can wander at will rather than being restrained as in a stall.

Loriner The maker of bits, spurs and all metal parts of the harness used for riding and driving.

Lungeing The process of schooling a young horse on a long rein attached to the noseband of a special cavesson (a bitless bridle). The horse circles the person holding the lunge rein at the required pace, demanded by voice.

Mane The long hair that grows down one or other side of the neck from the crest to the withers.

Manger The receptacle in the stable used for feeding the horse.

Mare The female of the horse species over four years of age.

Martingale Various different forms exist of this piece of harness, usually used as some form of restraint.

Muck out The act of cleaning out the stable daily to ensure a fresh, healthy bed for the horse.

Nap When a horse refuses to do as required by its rider, a nappy horse is one that is thoroughly disobedient.

Navicular An incurable disease of the navicular bone, almost always in the front feet. It results in acute lameness.

Near side The left side of the horse, from which side it is customary to mount and lead a horse.

New Zealand rug A form of rug with a waterproof canvas outside and rugging inside, used to turn horses out in winter if they are clipped or if the weather is bad.

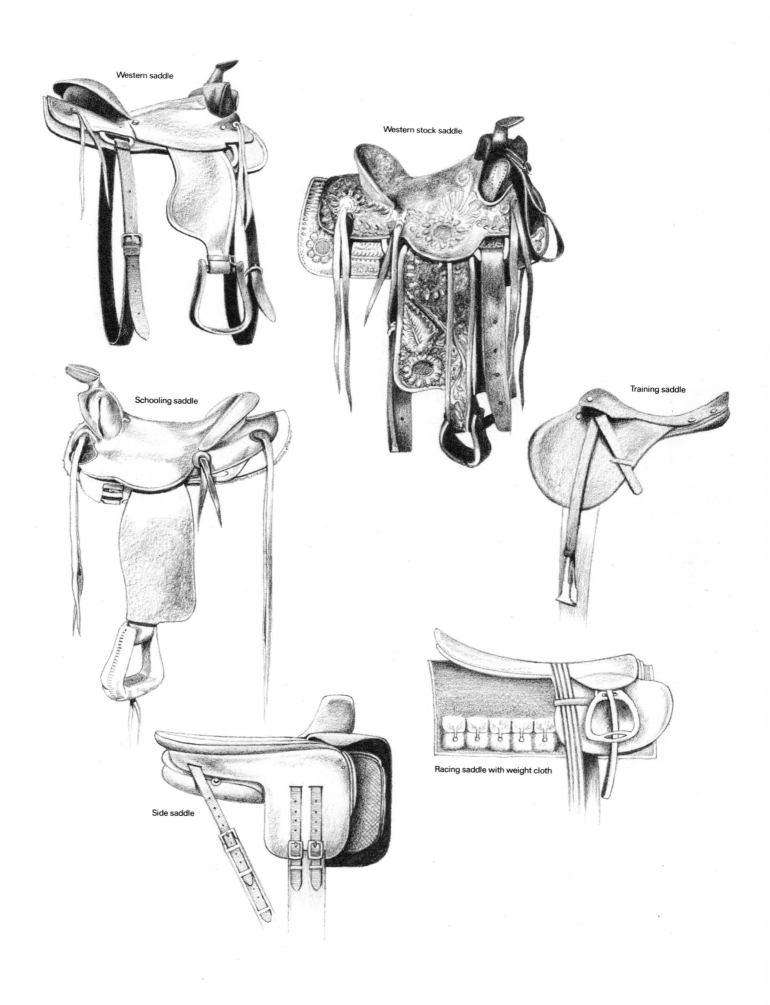

Western saddle

Western stock saddle

Schooling saddle

Training saddle

Side saddle

Racing saddle with weight cloth

Noseband The leather band that forms part of the bridle and which is fixed around the horse's nose. There are various forms of noseband, some acting as extra restraint on the horse, like a drop noseband, a grakle, or Kineton.

Numnah Material cut to the shape of a saddle and placed underneath it to prevent chafing.

Oats The main grain that is fed to horses. Care is necessary when judging the proper amount to give, as oats can be very overheating and make a horse too excitable.

Opening meet The first meeting of the hunting season, usually at the beginning of November.

Over-reach A faulty action when the hind toe clips the front heel, often causing injury.

Palomino A colour rather than a breed of horse, it is a beautiful golden shade made all the more striking as it is accompanied by a creamy mane and tail.

Pelham A type of bit that includes a curb chain.

Piaffe Often described as 'trotting on the spot', piaffe is an advanced dressage movement.

Piebald A term that describes the colour of a horse with both black and white markings on the body.

Plaits A decorative way of tying the hair of the mane and tail. It is seen most often in horses groomed for the show ring and out hunting and serves no purpose other than to make the horse look more beautiful.

Point to Points Races run by hunts and confined to horses that have qualified to run by being hunted for a specific length of time during the preceeding season. The races are run over brush fences, similar to steeplechasing.

Pony A small horse which does not exceed 14.2hh. in height at maturity.

Rearing A very dangerous vice when the horse stands upright on its back legs. A horse is then likely to fall over backwards.

Roller A form of girth used to keep stable rugs in place.

Rubber Stable rubber is a cloth used for final polishing of the horse after thorough grooming to remove the final layer of dust and grease.

Saddle This forms the main part, together with the bridle, of a horse's equipment for riding. It takes various styles, the most popular being a general purpose which can be used for ordinary riding, hunting, jumping while specialized saddles can be obtained for dressage, racing, show jumping and side-saddle.

Sand crack A dry crack that forms in the wall of the horse's hoof; it can be eradicated by careful treatment from the farrier.

Slug A term used to describe a lazy horse.

Snaffle The mildest form of bit to put in a horse's mouth, provided it is smooth.

Sock The white marking on a leg extending from the coronet a short way up the leg. A longer marking is known as a stocking.

Splint A bony growth that often forms on a young horse's front leg on the splint bone. It may cause temporary lameness, but after a time this will disappear.

Stirrup Iron The metal fitting for the rider's foot when mounted. It is attached to the saddle via the stirrup leather which fits on to a bar on the side of the saddle.

Tack Slang name for the equipment used on a horse: saddle, bridle, etc.

Thrush A disease of the feet caused through neglect in cleaning out the hoof. Easily recognizable from the foul-smelling discharge that is present.

Tree The basis on which all saddles are constructed. May be metal, wooden or more recently fibre glass.

Trot The two-time pace of the horse when the legs move diagonally.

Vice Vices in horses are objectionable habits, often dangerous to horse and rider – as in rearing, shying, bucking; or injurious to the health of the horse – as in wind-sucking, weaving, crib-biting etc.

Weaving A nervous habit that becomes a vice. The horse transfers its weight alternatively from one foot to the other and weaves its head back and forth over the stable door, losing condition and often passing the habit on to other horses.

Whip There are various forms of this aid, including cutting, hunting, dressage, show cane, and driving.

Wisp A plait of hay made to muscle up and tone the horse, during grooming.

Withers The point at which the neck of the horse joins the back above the shoulder. Horses are measured from the ground to the withers.

Worms All horses carry worms and it is only by a regular programme of dosing that they can be kept under control. If allowed to get out of hand, the horse rapidly loses condition and death may result.

Index

Acknowledgments

The publishers would like to thank the following organizations and individuals for their kind permission to reproduce the photographs in this book:

Ackermann: 178 below; AFA Colour Library: 37, 135 above; Ardea Photographics: 11 below, 35, 44–45, 46, 47; Barnaby's Picture Library: 173; Budd Studio: 165 below; John Carnemola: 170, 174 above and below; Bruce Coleman Ltd: (R Meeke) 166, (Hans Reinhard) 33, 40–41, 62 , 124, (Joe van Wormer) 161; Colour Library International: 128; Courtauld Institute of Art; 178 above; Gerry Cranham: 108 above, 115; Anne Cumbers: 56, 76–77, 123; Daily Telegraph Colour Library: 7 below, 34 above, 53 below, 64 above, 64–65, 97, 98, 104 above, 111, 118, 121 below, 122, 134 below, 135 below left, 171 above and below, 176; James Fain Logan: 162 above and below, 165 above; Graham Finlayson: 4–5, 13 above and below, 38, 39 below, 67, 69, 70 above, 71 above, centre and below, 72–73, 108, 127, 130–131, 143 below; Fotofass: 34 below; Robert Harding Associates: 10, 40, 163 above; Hoof and Horns: 172; E D Lacey: 102, 103 above and below, 104 below, 106, 107, 110; Keystone Press Agency: 48; Mansell Collection; 179; John Moss: 66, 80 above and below; NHPA (H R Allen) 126 below, 136–137; Photo Library of Australia: 175; Pictor: 14, 36, 52, 58, 59 above, 79, (FPG) 167; Picturepoint: 9, 116–117, 169; Popperfoto: 135 below right; Peter Roberts: 7 above, 39 above, 72, 100 below, 109; Ianthe Ruthven: 2–3, 6; Spectrum: 8, 16 below, 42, 43 above and below, 50, 51, 59 below, 63 below, 75; Tony Stone Associates: 65 right, 68; Sally Anne Thompson: 11 above, 12, 57, 61, 70 below, 74, 101, 125, 126 above, 129 above and below, 133 above, centre left and centre right, 136, 140 right, 164; Don Walker, Appaloosa Horse Club: 63 above, 168; Elisabeth Weiland: 1, 15, 49, 53 above, 60, 64 below, 99, 100 above, 105 left and right, 120 above, centre and below, 121 above, 132, 134 above, 138, 139, 140 left, 141, 142, 143 above, 144, 163 below; ZEFA (B Benjamin) 54–55, (Wolfgang Fritz) 119, (Gerolf Kalt) 114, (Oechstein) 16 above, (R G Theissen) 112–113.